Thomas Taylor Allen

The life of Armelle Nicolas

a peasant by birth

Thomas Taylor Allen

The life of Armelle Nicolas
a peasant by birth

ISBN/EAN: 9783741156168

Manufactured in Europe, USA, Canada, Australia, Japa

Cover: Foto ©Thomas Meinert / pixelio.de

Manufactured and distributed by brebook publishing software
(www.brebook.com)

Thomas Taylor Allen

The life of Armelle Nicolas

THE LIFE OF
ARMELLE NICOLAS

A PEASANT BY BIRTH
BY OCCUPATION A SERVANT
commonly called
"THE GOOD ARMELLE"
in her ineffable converse with God
"THE DAUGHTER OF LOVE"

TRANSLATED FROM THE FRENCH
BY
THOMAS TAYLOR ALLEN
(Translator of "The Autobiography of Madame Guyon")

WITH INTRODUCTORY LETTER BY THE LATE
PROF. EDWARD DOWDEN

LONDON: H. R. ALLENSON, LIMITED
RACQUET COURT, FLEET STREET, E.C.

INTRODUCTORY LETTER BY PROFESSOR DOWDEN

TRINITY COLLEGE
DUBLIN, *March 17th*, 1899

MY DEAR ALLEN,

I have read with great interest your reduced translation of the Life of *La bonne Armelle*. The reduction I am sure is judiciously made, and as to your work as translator you have been most happy in preserving the character of the original, in which deep things are recorded with a kind of ardent simplicity.

The question of the authorship, whether by the Ursuline nun or with a rehandling by Dom Echallard, hardly entered into my consideration as I read. I took the book as a thing lived and made out of life by somebody and, as such, having in all that is best its own self-verification.

It is certainly remarkable that such a book should now have passed so much out of sight. I know your *Mme Guyon*, of course, and *St Teresa's Autobiography*, and *St John of the Cross*;

v

and it seems to me that in *La bonne Armelle*
(especially in the later chapters) are things as
true and as beautifully said as in any of these
other books. It lacks no doubt the historical
interest connected with persons known to all the
world and influential through the foundation of
Houses, or the strife of prelates. But its very
humbleness in outward circumstance gives it a
peculiar place of its own. The life of a domestic
servant, who did her household work faithfully,
yet who became the subject and scene of inner
experience so wonderful, is distinguished by its
very modesty of circumstance.

Although now and again something occurs
which is specially related to Roman Catholicism,
in essentials the book transcends any single
communion, or Church, and belongs to every one
who has heard the same voice that Armelle heard.
There are pages for which I do not care, in which
descriptions are attempted, by imagery or otherwise, of what cannot be described ; but that is the
case with other books of the group to which this
belongs. In that group I think it takes a worthy
place by virtue of its best chapters—those to
which the other chapters form the natural and
necessary introduction—and perhaps, by virtue
of the obscurity of Armelle's outward life, it takes
a unique place. The disinterestedness of love,

the supersession of self, the union of what is above self, are expressed with a beautiful sincerity of experience which is not surpassed in books more famous.

I hope you will carry out your intention of publishing it. Readers for it there must be, though I cannot guess whether they would be many or few.

Sincerely yours,

EDWARD DOWDEN

TRANSLATOR'S PREFACE

THE name of the subject of this Biography is probably entirely unknown to the English-speaking world notwithstanding the wide popularity of the work when it appeared in France. Printed for the first time in 1676, five years after the death of Armelle, the third edition, from which this translation has been made, appeared at Cologne in 1704 after careful corrections by the celebrated Peter Poiret. It was translated into German and published in 1708, with a second edition in 1719. There appears also to have been a Dutch translation issued. In English a short account of Armelle was given in a pamphlet by the anonymous Bristol translator of *Madame Guyon's Life* in 1772.

This Life, mainly autobiographical, was compiled by an Ursuline nun known as Jeanne of the Nativity under the circumstances detailed in a Prefatory Letter to the Superior and members of her Community. She had become intimately attached to Armelle during the latter's service at their Convent, and in repeated conversations

learned from her the previous experiences she
had passed through. A subsequent order from
the Spiritual Director required Armelle to open
herself fully to this friend. The Superior and
others requested Jeanne to commit to writing
the valuable materials she had acquired that
others also might be edified, but distrusting her
own abilities and wanting leisure, Jeanne long
hesitated and postponed the task. At last, owing
to their urgency and an interior movement, she
could not resist. " On Christmas Eve 1650 I
withdrew into my cell," she says, " and prayed
Our Lord that if it was his will he would be
pleased to furnish the matter and suitable con-
ceptions, for as for myself I had none, and knew
not how to begin. After that I set myself to
write, and this I did with such facility that the
pen could hardly follow the thoughts of my mind,
so that before going to Matins I had finished the
first chapter without any further industry or
application on my part than the simple expression of matters that presented themselves to
my thought." Thus nine or ten chapters were
written when a doubt as to whether her memory
was trustworthy perplexed her and she feared to
consult Armelle for its resolution, lest the humility
of the latter should revolt at the project. This
difficulty was removed by Armelle herself who,

having entered on a still deeper state of spiritual
life, was impelled to wish that others also should
learn her experiences "that after her death God
might be praised, loved, and thanked." Finding
her in this disposition, the chapters already written
were read over for her correction, and the rest of
the work was similarly completed practically from
her dictation.

Barbier [1] is disposed to throw a doubt on this
authorship, suggesting one Dom Olivier Echallard,
a Benedictine, as the real compiler; but I have
been unable to discover any foundation for this
surmise.

The various letters and authorizations prefixed
to Poiret's edition, emanating as they do from the
Higher Church dignitaries of the province where
she lived, and written at the time of Armelle's
decease, seem to me conclusive. In the original
the work consists of over eight hundred close
printed pages divided into two books—the first,
narrative, the second mainly didactic, illustrating
the saintly character of Armelle as possessor of
each Christian virtue. I can well believe that
the whole work was carefully revised and perhaps
this second book composed by another hand than
the Ursuline nun; but the narrative and the
details of Armelle's experiences are, I believe, as

[1] *Dictionnaire des ouvrages anonymes*, Paris, 1872.

.stated, the faithful record of Armelle's own account taken down by her sympathizing friend. In cutting down the vast bulk I have given only a few paragraphs from the second book, and reduced the first book by omitting certain repetitions and comments for which the compiler, not Armelle, is responsible. I have been careful to preserve entire, with little exception, Armelle's experiences related in Armelle's own words.

To understand such experiences is beyond the scope of metaphysics and modern philosophy ; the seeing eye needs neither to perceive the sun shining before it. Let the candid inquirer study Plato's simile of the dwellers in the den and open his mind to receive it as a simple statement of actual fact. The percipient in man is not this or that organ, nor yet the totality of those organs, but the central spirit (pneuma), which muffled up at present in psyche and body is thus cut off from cognizance of the external world save through the avenues of those organs. But when through any cause the pressure of these mufflers is relaxed, or by superior illumination the spirit is enabled to transcend them, its inherent power of perception is enjoyed with a certainty and conviction of truth that nothing can disturb.

An illustration of the true nature of man, as spirit muffled by psyche and body, may be found in an electric lamp with the incandescent centre surrounded by an opal shade and a green outer covering.

From the earliest times such illuminés have not been wanting in the Christian community. With these there is nothing in the nature of historical development, each one has for herself had the barriers removed and gazed upon the True Light, while Confessors and Spiritual Directors have collected and endeavoured to systematize in terms of the intellect the ex- periences related by their penitents. With these systems [1] the late Bampton Lectures on Christian Mysticism deal in a sympathetic spirit ; but wide is the difference between such second-hand learned treatises and the direct experiences of the Saint whose spirit eye has been opened to see. "Many the thyrsus bearers but few the true Mystics."

The word Mystic or Mysticism to the aver- age educated Englishman suggests from mere similarity of sound something of mistiness and obscurity, whereas its real significance is the direct contrary. The Mystic is he who has been initiated into reality, while fools run about the world swayed by mere opinion—the man whose soul has been illuminated by the true sun of the upper world, while the denizens of the cave he

[1] This Preface was written about 1899.

has left employ themselves in guessing the
sequence and relations of mere shadows, thrown
upon a wall by the torch-light of sensual reason.
The French *illuminé* far more accurately repre-
sents the ancient use of the word ; but among
the Roman Catholics they are generally styled
spiritual writers, or writers on the interior way.
Whatever the name, however, the important
fact to be remembered is that the subject dealt
with is reality, as opposed to phenomena, with
which alone the physical and psychic worlds make
us acquainted. It is no mere quickening of the
imagination or intellect which takes place when
the Divine Spirit has been allowed to enter the
centre of the human spirit (pneuma) ; but the
substance of the human pneuma is then actually
changed—vivified and made infinitely brighter
by the influx and the assimilation of the Divine
substantial effluence infused ; and this change
manifests itself primarily through the Will, in
a complete change of purpose and motive. The
whole conduct of life is altered ; what before was
sought eagerly is scorned and rejected ; what
was rejected with scorn is eagerly sought.
Nothing is more practical and purposeful than
the lives of the most eminent Saints. Consider
the two Catherines, of Sienna and of Genoa ;
St Theresa, Madam Guyon, and others—frail

women in weak health, who went through toils
that would have exhausted strong men, and exhibited an activity and energy that would have
done credit to famous Captains.

The activity and energy of St Paul are a
favourite subject of comment : those named
above, his followers, in that like him, through
the extinction of self, they could say, as he did,
" I live, yet not I, Christ lives in me," were in
no way behind in practical efficiency, according
to the measure each received.   Not in metaphysic
subtleties of the Intellect, nor in vivid play of
the Imagination, but in self-sacrificing service
for others does the illuminated and vivified spirit
employ them.   William Law's definition of the
Mystic will not be inappropriate here.

" Tho' if a man was to be told what is meant
by a Mystical Divine he must be told of something
as heavenly, as great, as desirable, as if he was
told, what is meant by a real, regenerate, living,
member of the Mystical Body of Christ.

.   .   .   .   .

" You will perhaps say, Do I then call all the
world to these Spiritual Books ?   No, by no
means.   But, I call all those whom our Saviour
called to himself in these words : Come unto me
all ye that labour and are heavy laden, and I will
refresh you."

Many such there surely are in this age of pessimism when " le savant nie, la prêtre doute," while the would-be practical guides can offer no better gods for vulgar adoration than Mammon and Belial (which indeed only *too universally* are worshipped in " *spirit and in truth* ") ; and it is to them this little book is offered. In it they will see how the lowest domestic drudgery may be exalted to a dignity above that of the highest rank in State or Church, for " Where the Spirit of the Lord is there is liberty," and " the Spirit of the Lord giveth light and understanding to the simple." Here too they will learn that the way thereto is through Fidelity—the honestly discharging the duty at hand as in the presence of God, trusting all to His loving care.

It is possible some readers may be offended by the reference to Purgatory and the interest Armelle took in her " poor brothers." A few explanations on the subject may be useful.

A German proverb says that in emptying the dirty water from the bath one should be careful not to throw out the baby also. It would perhaps have been well had the Protestant Reformers borne it in mind when dealing with the Romish doctrine of Purgatory. Whatever the corruptions and scandals that had accreted,

[1] Letter to Dr Trapp.

there was a foundation of truth beneath, which unfortunately was then rejected. Madame Guyon thus explains the doctrine in its highest form.

Speaking of lost souls, she writes : " That it is not God who rejects them, by a volition of rejecting them, or by hatred, but by necessity, that in God the unchangeableness of love is entire for the sinner, so that, as all the cause of that rejection is in the sinner, God cannot receive him into his Grace until the cause of this rejection ceases. Now this cause does not subsist in the effect of sin, but in the will and inclination of the sinner ; so that as soon as this will and inclination ceases on the side of the sinner, however foul and horrible he may be, God purifies him by His charity and love and receives him into His grace : but as long as there remains in the man the will to sin, although from powerlessness, or lack of opportunity he does not commit the sin he wills, it is certain he would be rejected from God, owing to this perverse will. . . . If this sinner die during the time that his will is rebellious and turned towards sin, as death fixes for ever the disposition of the soul, and the cause of his impurity is still subsisting, this soul can never be purified by the Charity of God, and can consequently never be received into Him ; so that his damnation is eternal. . . . But

b

if this sinner die penitent—that is to say, that the cause (which is the will to sin, is removed, and only the effect remains, which is the impurity caused by sin), however horrible and filthy the sinner may be, he ceases to be a sinner, although he does not cease to be filthy. He is then in a state to be purified. God by an infinite charity has provided a bath of love and justice, but a painful bath, to purify this soul : that bath is Purgatory, which is not in itself painful, yet is so in the cause of the pain, which is impurity."

This statement of the doctrine substantially agrees with what Swedenborg, a man who had not the least sympathy with, or respect for, the Romish Church, declares to have been ascertained by him in his transcendental experiences. He, while fully recognizing the intermediate state between the life on this physical plane and the permanent state of spirit existence, is not always consistent with himself, and though knowing nothing of the ecclesiastical distinction between sins Venial and sins Mortal, he yet maintains that the direction taken in this life, whether upward or downward, must continue unaltered in the next state : so that those who have honestly struggled against their vices, even unsuccessfully, on earth will continue that struggle in the next stage until they are finally helped upwards to reach the highest heavens ; those, on the contrary, who have resisted all control and set themselves to work iniquity with set design and deliberate choice, having there full scope to gratify their bent and necessarily associating with others of a similar kidney, will then pursue the downward course with an accelerated velocity until they find themselves ultimately in the lowest Hell. Of a class between the two, who in this life are seesawing between the upward and downward course, he will not hear—every one on earth, he maintains, is progressing in the one or other direction. This comes to very much the same thing as the view explained by Madame Guyon.

It remained for modern Spiritualism, ridiculed and decried as it is by ignorance and prejudice, to introduce a system of ideas philosophically coherent and far more consonant to the relations which reason insists must exist between the Father of all and the children he has given birth to. The Gospel tells us that " God is Love "— and Plato in the *Timæus* had previous to that taught the heathen world that the motive of Creation was the Goodness of God. He willed, as it were, to multiply himself; but as this was impossible to be done in his Infinity, he called into being Finite creatures, to express, each according to his form, the perfections of Divine

b *

Love and Wisdom. The first condition of their
doing so was that they should be self moved, that
is finding their principle of action from within :
not moved *ab externo* like inert matter. In that
inmost centre of their being he designed to make
his seat, and in proportion as they drew from this
well of spiritual life, their capacities would be
enlarged until they approximated ever more and
more to the Infinity of himself.

Love never seeks anything for itself—to pour
itself out in blessing its object is the very essence
of its being. To bless with pouring into them
the fulness of his perfections and happiness is the
one and only mind that God could by any possi-
bility have ever had towards any of the creatures
whose end and destiny was, and is, to be the willing receptacles of that fulness. They, through the
freedom of will with which they were endowed,
have the ability to shut the door against those
blessings ; but Love will not be baffled, and will
ultimately find the means of abating that self-
will without ever violating its essential freedom.
With truth Law in his "Spirit of Love" speaks
of "that adorable Deity, whose infinite being is
an infinity of mere love, an unbeginning, never-
ceasing, and forever overflowing ocean of meekness,
sweetness, delight, blessing, goodness, patience,
and mercy ; and all this as so many blessed

streams breaking out of the abyss of universal love. Father, Son, and Holy Ghost, a triune infinity of love and goodness, for ever and ever, giving forth nothing but the same gifts of light and love, of blessing and joy, whether before or after the fall, either of angels or men."

It may seem strange to some that I should couple Spiritualism with such a man as Law, but in its way it is doing the same work as he strove to do. Adopting the experimental methods of materialism and physical science, it is proving, as against materialists and sham scientists, that man persists when the physical instrument, through which he at present acts, has decayed; and as against the retailers of ancient tradition and scholastic dogmatism, that morally as he was at death, so he continues after the laying aside his mortal vesture. The conditions of his existence are altered; he, in his essential character, bent, and purpose, remains unaltered. What the body is to him on this plane, the psyche is to him then; and the externals with which he finds himself then surrounded and limited are similarly in relation to the powers of the psyche as the physical limitations of earth are to the earthly body. But the powers of the psyche are vastly greater than when muffled and dulled by its instrument

of clay. No longer so limited, the Will and
Imagination of the psyche can now give an ob-
jective existence to the forms of the desires; the
psyche creates its own externals, and herein lies
the great difficulty of the change in direction,
which Swedenborg thought impossible, for a
man who has sold himself "to work all un-
cleanness with greediness."

He associates with his like; on earth, good
and bad are mingled together, and laws, public
opinion, etc., impose some restraint; at least
on the external behaviour of the worst. But on
the psychic stage, unless his anti-social crimes
have developed an atmosphere (as in the case of
a murderer) which cuts him off in isolation and
darkness, he has full scope and no let from
his fellows for pursuing his downward course.
The penalty he no doubt reaps; the little light
still in him becomes darkened, the gnawing of
want bites deeper as each lawless desire gratified
leaves a greater void of dissatisfaction—the thirst
increases with drinking, the lust is inflamed,
not satisfied, by its indulgence, and each such act,
instead of being accompanied with a pleasurable
sensation, as on earth, where in the physical
economy the desire is coupled with a use, brings
nothing but a pang of torture. In this depth of
misery ever deepening, of darkness ever thicken-

ing, and of powerlessness ever increasing—even here they are not forgotten, and the instruments of their deliverance are already being prepared, to be applied whenever the Will has been so broken as to consent to guidance.

But the vast majority who leave earth are not of this type, they are rather undeveloped than wicked, and it is with such for the most part that spiritualism is conversant. Of those who on earth have resolutely struggled to live the better life, to subordinate the flesh to the spirit, to take up the yoke of Him " who is meek and lowly in spirit," and " bearing the cross daily to follow Him "—of such it can tell us nothing. Yet they are not indifferent to our struggles here, or to the misery and helplessness of their brothers in the Abyss of darkness. From among their ranks go forth the volunteers, who, filled with the Spirit of the Saviour, extend the hand of help, wherever a ray of human affection still survives, to draw forth from their misery those unable to help themselves.

Of that great day of Consummation, when the physical and psychic worlds shall be filled with the knowledge of God and all the hells shall have been emptied of their slaves—and perhaps even Satan, finding his occupation gone, shall confess himself vanquished, and fallen angels submit to

be blessed by the Infinite Love that called them
into existence for no other end : what shall I
say ? Only this : that he who knows the Love
of God as I do looks forward to see it.

I will close these considerations, meant not
for the self-satisfied many, treading the broad
road of routine—slaves of opinion ; but for the
earnest few—candid seekers, " who have ears
to hear "—with the answer which Armelle received to her perplexed prayer for the abolition
of sin : " That it was a decree given in the
tribunal of his divine Wisdom that men should
continue in the free unfettered choice to love him
or to offend him ; and that according to that
decree he could not force them, nor violate their
freedom ; but that he would draw them to him
by the chains of his love."

Three hundred years before Armelle the same
in substance had been the answer our Saviour
condescended to give the holy anchorite Mother
Juliana of Norwich : " Sin is behoveful " [that is
needful for the manifestation designed by God),
" but all shall be well, and all shall be well and
all manner of thing shall be well " ; and again
another time, " And thou shalt see thyself that
all manner of things shall be well."

CONTENTS

CHAPTER I

CHAPTER VI

CHAPTER VII

CHAPTER VIII

CHAPTER IX

CHAPTER X

CHAPTER XI

CHAPTER XII

Contents

CHAPTER XX

CHAPTER XXI

CHAPTER XXII

CHAPTER XXIII

CHAPTER XXIV

CHAPTER XXV

CHAPTER XXVI

CHAPTER XXVII

ARMELLE NICOLAS

CHAPTER I

THIS blessed woman was born the 19th September 1606 in the Parish of Campeneac, near the town of Ploermel, in the Bishopric of St Malo. Her father was George Nicolas and her mother Frances Neant. They were moderately well off for their rank, which was that of peasants, but strong in the fear of God and much inclined to his holy service. Among her father's good qualities, his devotion was such that he spent the greater part of Festivals and Sundays in prayer while he walked about his land, in order to avoid the company and debauchery of his neighbours. He was once chosen Vestryman of his Church, and he used to call that year the happiest of his life, for never was his heart so contented. Her mother on her side endeavoured to second the good inclinations of her husband, and thus they lived very peacefully to the edification of their neighbours.

God blessed their marriage by the birth of this virtuous daughter, who was followed by another and by four boys. She was named Armelle at

A   1

the Baptismal font, and from her tender youth
it appeared that God had chosen her in a special
manner to make manifest in her the effects of
his grace and of his love, for she was endowed
with an excellent disposition, a solid judgment,
a temper sweet and sociable, and an outward
carriage so balanced and reserved that modesty
appeared in all her actions. This made her so
amiable to all her relatives and others that she
was universally cherished and caressed by all,
but especially by her mother, who had for her
much tenderness.

As soon as she could speak she taught her the
Pater and *Ave* and other prayers, in which the
little one took a singular pleasure, finding nothing
more agreeable than praying to God. From an
early age it appeared she had an inclination for
solitude and silence ; and consequently, when a
little grown, her mother used to send her to look
after the sheep and other cattle, the occupation
which pleased her most, because she was there
alone by herself, far from the noise of the house,
and had leisure to repeat her chaplet and other
prayers, in which she spent the greater part of
the day, hid away in some corner of a hedge,
while her companions were engaged in playing
and amusing themselves. From this time Our
Lord commenced to draw her to himself by much

tenderness and sweetness, which he communicated to her in her little devotions.

One day when hid away as usual to say her prayers she found near her a cross to which was attached a crucifix by a little cord. Wondering who could have put it there she took it, kissed it, caressed it, and watered it with her tears, in great tenderness. At the height of her devotion the Devil, who already foresaw what was to happen, put into her mind that she ought not to do this, but on the contrary she ought to cast the crucifix to the ground, trample it under her feet and insult it. At the same time it seemed to her that some one tried to tear it from her hands, but she held firm and did not let go. Though these were only thoughts and suggestions without effect, she yet was so troubled at them, that she was beside herself, thinking she had committed a great sin, and she could find no rest until she had confessed. Although her Confessor assured her there had been no offence, for a long time after she could never think of it without shedding an abundance of tears.

Our Lord made use of this little circumstance, which was in reality nothing, to communicate to her great good ; for henceforth he imprinted on her heart a great tenderness of love and compassion for the tortures he had suffered on the

Cross, although she knew none in particular
except the five wounds of the feet, hands, and
side, which she henceforth every day devoutly
saluted with five *Paters* and five *Aves*. One day
conversing with her on the subject I asked who
had told her that Our Lord had received five
wounds. She answered me that she had noticed
them on this little crucifix ; and we may believe
that this did not happen by chance, but by a
secret disposition of Divine Providence, who
willed by such feeble commencements to open
an entrance for that great and burning love
which afterwards blazed up in the heart of his
faithful servant on contemplation of her Saviour's
sufferings.

When she was old enough for her first Communion she made every possible preparation for
it, and longed for the day when she was to receive
this great blessing. From the first time she received it, she found herself so smitten with love
and devotion to the holy Sacrament that she
would have wished to approach it every day,
had it been in her power. But as in the country
frequent Communions are not usual, she found
herself unable to give effect to her desire. The
older she grew the more this desire increased,
so that she watched for opportunities to satisfy
it. Whenever there was a Communion she was

one of the number ; and when it did not take place she used to ask some priest to give her the holy Communion where she would not be noticed. Indeed, there were some who of their own motion, or rather from that of God, invited her to it.

Among the graces which God bestowed on her in her tender youth, one of the most important from the effects it produced, was the giving her a clear knowledge of the sufferings of Souls in Purgatory. This knowledge was vividly impressed on her mind, without her knowing by whom, nor how : but she felt a great compassion for these poor Souls and a very great desire to be able to help them. Therefore all the good works she did, or the pains she endured, were all directed to that end. If in the heats of summer while minding her sheep she was oppressed by the heat, or by the cold in winter, she rejoiced that by this means she might relieve her brothers (for thus she used to call the Souls in Purgatory). If she had to sweep, or perform the hardest work in the house, it was with the same intention. Often she exposed herself to the heat of the sun, or to that of a great fire, holding out as long as she could, in order to diminish what they endure. At her meals she deprived herself of what she liked best, often of everything, to give it in alms to the poor, with this same intention. She used

to say to herself as a stimulus to helping them,
" If I saw one of my relations in a great fire from
which he could not get out, and that I was able
to get him out, should I not be very cruel to
leave him burn there and suffer ? How much
more then should I assist the Souls of my own
brothers, who are cruelly tormented and cannot
help themselves."

This consideration and reasoning, so much
beyond her age, or the instruction she could have
received from men, animated her so strongly in
the desire of assisting these poor Souls, that she
would willingly have allowed herself to be torn
in pieces for this purpose, and the compassion
she then conceived for their pains lasted throughout her whole life. She recognized it as a signal
benefit from the goodness of God to her, which
had drawn down great blessings on her soul, and
often she declared she had received great succour
and assistance from God by the aid of those Souls
she had succoured through her prayers ; and she
used to say that they were the cause of her happiness and the ground why God had so specially
attracted her to his divine service. While she
was so helpful to the deceased, she was not less
so to the living, whom she helped and served to
the utmost of her power, with great affection and
charity. All in her house loved her and turned

to her in all their needs. She had a great respect for her father and mother, to whom she was always so obedient that she never caused them the smallest displeasure. They therefore loved her more than their other children.

When she was about twenty-one years of age they wished to marry her, but she would not listen to it, and seeing herself often urged and besides obliged sometimes to be amongst persons too free, and void of that reserve to her taste, she began to weary of the country and was unable to rest quietly there. Another motive which contributed further to this unrest was the desire she had of receiving the little scapulary of the Holy Virgin and assisting in the Processions and other devotions that were practised every month in the church of the Carmelites of Ploermel, which she had heard spoken of. This desire was so keenly impressed on her mind that she thought of nothing else, and all her prayers and devotions had this in view. She therefore sought every opportunity of going to dwell in the town.

CHAPTER II

AFTER she had passed the earlier years in the house of her parents and gained by her virtues the goodwill and friendship not only of her relatives, but of some other persons in the neighbourhood, who were greatly edified by her modesty and reserve, a worthy lady who had a great regard for her desired to take her into service, and to this effect asked her from her parents with great urgency. At first they would not listen to it, but afterwards seeing that this lady still insisted on having her, and besides that their daughter showed great unrest in the country, they consented, although with regret, as well at being deprived of her as for the services she rendered in the household.

God made use of this opportunity to fulfil her desire to go and live in the town, where her mistress immediately took her. While there, at first she found herself very well off, apparently delivered from a great burden, in being no longer obliged on Festivals and Sundays to take part in dances and assemblies which are usual in the country, where sometimes her companions took

her as if by force. For always she had a great
aversion to them. Besides, she had the means
of often attending Mass and Preachings, and took
a great delight in hearing the word of God, to
which she was most attentive.

On the other hand her mistress was so satisfied with her and her services that she cherished
and loved her as her own daughter and gave
her every comfort possible, never finding fault,
except for the one thing that she worked too
hard. Indeed, she was unwearied at work, as
she had a large body, healthy, strong, and robust,
with an active mind, and did as much work as two.

It seemed that, things being thus, nothing
would have been able to make her desire to leave
a place where she had everything to her heart's
content ; nevertheless, she was not long there
before all this good treatment became matter of
disgust. Weariness and sadness seized upon her
so powerfully that she knew not what to do ;
everything became a source of pain. The more
she was cherished, caressed, and well treated,
the more she found discontent within herself,
without knowing any reason for it, except that
everything was to her disagreeable and insupportable.

In these circumstances her father died, and her
mistress allowed her to go for a few days to con-

sole her mother and settle matters, enjoining her
to return as soon as possible, for she so loved her
that she could not get on without her. She
returned therefore, but with great trouble and
difficulty ; however, as she had commenced her
second year of service she did what she could to
finish it, after which she asked for her discharge,
that she might return into the country. Her
mistress, unwilling to lose such a good and faithful
servant, did all she could to keep her, offering an
increase of wages and to relieve her of part of the
work of the house if she would remain. But she
could not make up her mind to it, although
according to reason and her feelings she would
have wished to do so. An interior influence
that she did not understand drew her elsewhere,
and so she left her good mistress and returned
to her relatives, who were very glad to see her
again, while she was still more so at having
left the town, thinking she had left there her
distress and oppression of mind.

She was not a month in the country when
she changed her opinion. For many reasons it
became insupportable to her, besides the interior
oppression which increased every day ; for when
there, her relatives urged her again with importunity to marriage. Moreover, she was compelled often to see much licentiousness among

young people, who had no respect for decency of
life. This she could not endure, and, moreover,
she had not the advantage of hearing holy Mass
or of Communicating as often as she used to do
in the town; so that to avoid all these incon-
veniences she again obtained the permission of
her relatives to return to the town, after having
remained about four months in the country under
a strange oppression of mind.

Immediately on her return to the town three
or four persons wanted to have her in their service,
for the lady she had lived with had been so satisfied that there was competition as to who should
have her. She again entered a house, where
she was much loved and cherished, notwithstanding which, she remained there only three weeks,
when she was constrained to leave, owing to the
insupportable oppression she experienced, which
increased in proportion to the good treatment she
received. For the more easy her body, the more
her mind suffered. In less than three or four
months she was in two other houses, to see if she
could settle down, but she had to leave every
place, however much she wished to remain.
This caused her great trouble, as she did not
know or penetrate yet into the designs of Divine
Providence, who permitted it for her very great
benefit, as she afterwards recognized.

There was among the Carmelites of Ploermel a nun who had known formerly this worthy woman, and she wished to engage her in the service of her own sister, who was married in the town—a very virtuous lady, well disposed towards the service of God, who had asked her sister to speak to that effect. This nun sent for her and invited her to enter the service of her sister, not by promising her a fine time and little work, as had been done in other houses where they wished to engage her. On the contrary, she told her frankly that she would have a great deal of work, because another servant who had been there many years was about to leave in order to become a nun, and that all the work of the household, which was large, would fall on her, but that otherwise she would have every ground for satisfaction and contentment.

This proposal, more calculated to repel than to attract, she felt herself interiorly moved and strongly urged to accept, her opinion being that God let her know that this was the place where he wished her to be. She readily agreed then, and in truth we have well seen in the course of time that it was indeed the house in which from all eternity he had destined to bestow the graces and favours which he afterwards communicated to this holy Soul—house of blessing and sanctification for her, since it was there he drew her more specially to him, although from her childhood she was led to virtue. It was in this place she experienced trials and contradictions, infinitely more profitable than all the caresses she had received elsewhere, since they made her acquire the habit of the most solid virtues.

CHAPTER III

To confirm further this worthy woman in the thoughts she had had, that the will of God was for her to dwell in this house, he permitted that as soon as she entered it she found herself relieved of that oppression and trouble of mind she had hitherto suffered ; and she was so free and so happy that nothing could be more. Besides, her services and behaviour gave such satisfaction that no fault could be found. As to work, she had only to look after the children, for the project of the other servant had fallen through, and she remained in the house looking after the heavier work of the household.

God having thus disposed and ordered all things according to the designs of his eternal Providence, he commenced at the same time to put his hand to the work, and to cast the foundations of this high and grand edifice of perfection and to adorn and embellish that Temple, which his Majesty had reserved to be the throne of his love and the place of his dwelling and of his delight. For this purpose he made use of a way very common and usual in making Saints, namely,

14

the reading the Lives and actions of other Saints ;
for the custom in this house was, that every evening after supper there was reading in the Lives
of the Saints or some other spiritual book on
the same subject. This worthy woman was very
careful to be present, and took a singular pleasure
in hearing related the virtuous and heroic actions
of the Saints and admired all they had done for
God. As a consequence she was filled with an
ardent and strong desire to imitate them, and
she wished for and sought out every opportunity.
She was so preoccupied with this desire that day
and night she thought of nothing else but the
means of becoming like them.

But these great desires and ardours were only
small steps to the transports which afterwards
she experienced. As she had a taste for listening
to reading and that of the evening did not fully
satisfy her, she begged one of the girls of the
family, who has since become a nun of the Ursu-
lines in the same town, to read her something
from time to time. This the young lady willingly
did, and through the permission of God she one
day read to her a book which treated of the
Passion of our Lord and what he had suffered.

This was the book which completed the capture
of her heart, already so well disposed thereto.
It is impossible to tell the admirable effects that

this reading and knowledge operated in her soul,
which was thereby so shattered and inflamed
with love, that she was quite beside herself;
while at the same moment every idea of every
kind whatever was so banished from her mind,
that day and night there remained no other
object for her but that of the sufferings of her
Saviour. It caused her such grief and affliction
that she faded and withered from unhappiness,
as well at the extreme torments he suffered as
because her sins had been the cause. For at the
same time this was so visibly impressed on her
mind that she knew not what to do. The ardour
and distress were so great that she thought she
was in a consuming fire which every day increased
more and more.

While in this state, and not knowing to whom
to have recourse for enlightenment in a matter
so new and strange, God, who already held her
for his own, provided her with a person to serve
her as guide and conductor on the roads through
which he willed her to pass. It was a Carmelite
Father, a very holy monk, well understanding the
ways of the Spirit, to whom one day by chance
she went to Confession. After Confession she
felt strongly inspired to open to him the whole
state of her soul. She did so, relating how everything had happened and that she was at the

last point from the interior ardour she felt ; she
feared that there might be some artifice of the
Devil in these extraordinary effects and ardours
which were experienced ; although at the bottom
of her heart she was certain it proceeded from
God.

This Father after having heard and closely
examined her was immediately convinced that
God had great designs for this Soul, without,
however, declaring anything to her, or letting her
know that God was the author of what was taking
place in her. He merely encouraged her strongly
to be faithful to God and to give herself entirely
to his guidance, to avoid sin and to be faithful
to follow the movements of Grace. For his part
he offered to aid her in all he could, and told her
to come freely to see him whenever she had need
of his assistance. This she conformed to ever
since, doing nothing without the advice of this
good Father, as long as he was in the neighbourhood, and rendering prompt obedience to him in
all things—a virtue which she has always practised
towards those who have had the guidance of her
soul. From that time God gave her so great a
desire to allow herself to be guided by the will of
another, that she has always had this sentiment
in her heart, " Provided I do not do my own
will, it matters nothing to me ; let what will

B

happen, I shall distress myself for nothing. But,
if once I follow my own will, I hold myself for
lost.''

Being thus provided with a guide and docility
to follow his orders, and the thought of the
sufferings of the Saviour continuing to fill her
mind, the Incarnate Word communicated to her
sometime after an interior view, by which he
made known to her that it was not the Jews,
nor the executioners, who were the authors of his
death, but that the love alone which from all
eternity he had borne to her had attached him
to the Cross to deliver her from her sins. This
view so penetrated her heart and caused such
great love and such excessive contrition as can
hardly be expressed in words. When speaking
of this contrition she said, that the least sentiment she had of her sins was more than enough
to deprive her of a thousand lives, if she had
them, had not God by a special grace kept her.
The effects indeed which it produced show how
great it was.

For this view of her sins caused her so great
a hatred of herself that she would have liked to
cast herself into Hell to satisfy divine justice
and get rid of the sin, which had caused her
Saviour's death, and often when transported
out of herself by the force of love and sorrow

she used to say to God, " O my Lord, give me
rather death and hell than the view of your love
and my sins." She would have liked then to
suffer all the torments of the martyrs, and would
have desired to be cut, torn, burnt, reduced to
powder, to satisfy her love. When an opportunity of suffering offered she seized it with more
eagerness than a famished person does food, or
a heated stag plunges into the water ; for in truth
she was a-hungered and a-thirst for sufferings.
God on his part advancing his work gave every
day new motives for her contrition ; for he so
clearly represented to her mind in all minute
details the torments he had endured in his Passion,
and which hitherto she had been ignorant of
(having only a general knowledge of his having
died upon the Cross), that without any effort
on her part her mind was constantly accompany-
ing our Saviour in his torments.

At one time she saw him in the Garden of
Olives sweating his precious blood and praying
to his Father ; another time, taken by the Jews,
bound, dragged before Caiaphas and Herod ;
other times, buffeted, spit upon, torn with blows,
crowned with thorns ; in short, all the pains of
our Saviour, both exterior and interior, were as
fully represented to her as if she saw them with
her own eyes when he endured them ; and all

this with that interior voice crying aloud in the depth of her heart, " IT IS THE LOVE YOUR SAVIOUR BORE YOU WHICH CAUSED ALL THESE SUFFERINGS."

All this caused her such sorrow, and made her shed such tears, that every night she did nothing but groan and weep ; not venturing to do so by day, lest she should be observed, unless when she was alone. She shed tears, and in such abundance that her eyes were like inexhaustible springs. It was at this time God bestowed on her the gift of tears, which lasted all through her life, though from a different cause ; for during more than a year her tears were those of contrition and regret at having offended God, but afterwards they were tears of love.

To these views of the torments of our Lord was added a very special and marked one of his precious blood, for wherever she went, or whatever she did, she saw herself always as if bathed and sprinkled with this precious blood, and heard interiorly the words, " See'est thou this blood ? It was shed to make a bath to purify and cleanse thy soul." This so influenced her and threw her into such distress that she was intolerable to herself, and not without reason ; for, as she afterwards used to say, she must have been worse than the devils not to answer to such love.

All these things took place at the commence-

ment without the knowledge of any one save her
Confessor ; for our Lord gave her this grace that
all the favours he bestowed took effect interiorly,
and if at times anything appeared outwardly,
he permitted that no one paid attention, or it was
attributed to some other cause. For example,
her silence and great concentration and modesty
were regarded as ignorance or natural stupidity ;
besides, her condition as a servant made her escape
notice. But the principal reason was her constant
prayer to Our Lord, in which she very humbly
asked him " to keep her hid and covered under
the wing of his Providence as a chicken is under
that of its mother (these are her own words used
in prayer), and that she might be concealed and
unknown to any creature, except those who were
needed to aid her to love him the more, or who
would glorify his name for the graces he gave
her." This was her most usual prayer to God
at the commencement, and which he granted in
every particular, as well as the others he inspired
her to make to him.

She did not fail to make a faithful report of
her state to her Father Director, and he gave
advice suitable to the disposition of her heart,
without, however, assuring her that God was
acting directly in her. Often she was in doubt
as to the source of effects so extraordinary, and

this troubled her sometimes ; but he gave no other answer than that she should hope and trust herself to God, and that as long as her will was to serve him, his Majesty would never allow her to be deceived.

It was by a special providence of God that this worthy Father did not give her a full knowledge that all proceeded from him ; for had she known it and given herself up entirely to the sentiments she had, she would probably have died. Her nature was not yet capable of bearing such powerful efforts of grace ; but as she was never free from doubt this made her restrain herself, and the fear was the saving of her life, as she usually said in speaking of the early years, when Love made himself master of her heart. She used to thank God with great affection because by this means he had given her time to love him and serve him with more purity and perfection, for in all these excessive ardours she afterwards recognized there was a mixture of nature, and to purify her therefrom God allowed her soon after to pass through many trials and toils, as well from the devils as from other sources.

CHAPTER IV

IT is usual with great Souls to suffer much from the devils, and there are few saints, I believe, who have not experienced their rage and who are not indebted to the assaults, made with a view to their destruction, but which have had an effect quite the opposite to such malice. This has been very evident in the life of the blessed woman of whom we treat, for she suffered great temptations from them, which, nevertheless, through the goodness of our Lord, were very advantageous to her. After she had spent a little more than a year in those great ardours and extreme grief for her sins, God gave power to the Devil to exercise and to torment her with various kinds of temptations, more hateful to her than death; and as it is the Devil's part to oppose and frustrate the works of God as much as he can, he directed all his assaults to ruin and destroy what God had built up in this Soul, using for the purpose temptations directly opposed to the favours communicated to her.

In the first place, instead of that strong love she had felt hitherto for our Lord and what con-

cerned his service, he impressed on her heart, as
it were, a hatred and aversion to God, with a
certain scorn and such a great weariness of all
kinds of good works, that the least thing relating
to the practice of good was intolerable to her.

Secondly, all the grief and contrition she had
felt for her sins was taken away, so that at the
sight of them she was as if insensible ; and much
worse, for she seemed to feel a certain movement
of joy at having offended God and opposed his
adorable wills. From this ensued a rough combat, for seeing herself so miserable, rage and
despair of salvation seized her in such a strange
way, that she believed her loss as certain as if
she were already in Hell ; and her despair so
increased that she was continually tempted to
kill herself and care no more about her damnation.

Thirdly, to counteract the praise and blessings
she had so lovingly given our Lord she found
herself attacked by a spirit of blasphemy so
powerful that, make what efforts she would, she
could not at times hinder herself from uttering some words, specially against the adorable
Eucharist, and even at the very moment she was
about to receive it. This was one of her most
painful torments.

In the fourth place, all views and thoughts of
the sufferings of Our Lord were taken away from

her mind, and there did not remain an idea any more than if she had never heard of them ; instead of which she seemed to be always in the company of devils, who incessantly urged her to give herself up to them.

But to prevent her succumbing under the heavy weight of such furious assaults, his Majesty impressed in the depth of her heart a certain fear of offending him, which though imperceptible to sense was yet powerful enough to restrain her will from ever consenting to the suggestions of the Devil ; but, except for this, she was like a person entirely abandoned and in despair, and it was out of her power to produce the smallest act that would in the least have consoled or strengthened her.

All her refuge was in her Confessor, to whom she declared all her troubles, which he himself a little before had predicted would come. He had great compassion for her, and endeavoured to console and strengthen her, but most often, in vain ; for while he spoke the Devil troubled her imagination, so that she did not hear what he was saying ; or if she heard, it had no effect in relieving her. Moreover, she felt great difficulty in doing what he enjoined on her ; yet she punctually obeyed, whatever repugnance she had to it.

During five or six months that this crisis lasted

it was impossible for her to sleep at night, owing
to the terrible spectres with which the devils
troubled her, taking various horrible faces of
monsters, which sometimes seemed about to
devour her. She was so miserable that she
would have deemed it a lesser ill to be swallowed
by them than to bear the pains with which her
mind was agitated. Sometimes also they beat
and ill-used her strangely and made her cry out
aloud, at which her fellow-servant awoke, and
she helped to the best of her power, without its
being observed, or that any one in the house
except herself had any knowledge of what was
going on.

This storm was too furious to last long, and
it pleased our Lord to withdraw her from it
after she had been about five or six months in
this state. His Majesty had compassion on her
wretchedness and made shine in the depth of her
heart rays of his divine Light, by which all the
efforts of her enemies were dissipated. She then
clearly recognized that with the aid of grace she
could not only overcome all these temptations,
but, further, all that hell could direct against her.
One evening when she and that other maid had
retired to say some prayers before going to bed,
this poor woman in a moment found herself so
exercised by diabolic suggestions, that it seemed

all the devils had undertaken to overthrow her
utterly and to make her enter into pure despair.
She lost speech and performed the acts and
gestures of a true demoniac. The other maid
was almost fainting at seeing her in this state
and knew not what remedy to have recourse to :
and indeed she was incapable of receiving any,
save from him who never abandons his own in
the height of their temptations.

While she was in the extremity of her troubles
her companion, who was watching her, saw with
her bodily eyes as it were the face of our Lord,
who in a mild and loving manner drew near to
his dear spouse and covered her with the mantle
with which he was clothed, in sign that he took
her under his holy protection. He then disappeared, and at the same time she who had
seen it cried out to the other, " Courage, dear
Sister, fear not, for I have just this moment seen
our Lord take you under his defence and protection." As to her, she had perceived nothing ;
but at the moment our Lord had bestowed this
grace her heart was strengthened in such a way
that she declared, in reality a great power had
been poured into her soul, which had driven off
the devils, so that they left her in peace, and she
returned to herself.

But the devils did not allow themselves van-

quished for this stroke. They still continued
their attacks as before ; but that interior power,
which had been communicated to her, baffled
all assaults and gave her courage in the midst of
their greatest fury to say to them that, " in spite
of their rage she would be Jesus Christ's and
would fight under his banners as a good soldier
under that of his Captain, that she would van-
quish them and carry off the victory against their
malice." These words were uttered with great
. vehemence, as if another spirit than her own
had said them, and she knew well that the devils
conceived great rage and indignation, and that
their strength began to diminish and grow weak.

At last our Lord, willing to deliver her completely
from their pursuits and to give her a sensible
mark that they had abandoned this place, which
his Majesty destined for his dwelling, permitted
that one Sunday in Church at Vespers, a week
or fortnight after she had received this grace,
she was suddenly seized with a trembling and
great terror. At the same time there issued
from her brain a black and dense smoke, which
gave off such a smell that she was near dying,
and for about half an hour she was surrounded
with this stink, which was so unbearable that she
has since declared that the foulest stinks of this
world are pleasant in comparison of that. After

lasting the time mentioned it dissipated, and then her heart was so strengthened and changed that she began to defy the Devil and to laugh at his vain efforts, saying, " Thou thoughtest, Satan, to carry off the victory over me and to ravish me from him who has won me at the price of his blood ; but I laugh at thee and thy artifices and I defy thee ever to overcome me."

Then turning to her God she said with a heart full of gratitude, " O my God, you have broken my bonds ; you have delivered me from the servitude of my enemies ; therefore, my Love, will I serve you for ever, and will combat under your arms all the powers of hell."

Often afterwards he tried to attack her over again, and came to the assault with new powers, greater than the former ; but he gained only shame and scorn, so strengthened was her heart by divine grace, which these struggles had rendered her more capable of receiving. Thus the enemy was compelled to give way and allow her to enjoy in quiet the graces and merits these battles had gained for her.

One of the principal was, that God kindled again in her heart the burning fire of his divine Love, which the wind of these temptations had, as it were, extinguished, at least as far as senti-ment. He rekindled it, I say, with such impetu-

osity and vehemence that she seemed to herself
to be, both as to the exterior and the interior,
nothing but fire and flame ; and to this interior
fire was joined an ardent desire to unite herself
to God, such as no language could describe.
This divine arrow, which had pierced her heart,
caused her to be incessantly in pursuit of him
who had discharged it. Night and day she
sighed for him and groaned, without finding
respite or rest in anything in the world. Her
mind was so alienated and beside itself, that she
was like one out of her senses, and any one seeing
her would have thought her mad ; for not knowing where to catch him who had shattered her
heart, she often ran from room to room thinking
there to meet with him. Other times she cried
after him and called him with all her strength,
and love which possessed her made her utter
words and do things which would have passed
for extravagances and void of reason ; but not
beyond the height of her love.

At night it was impossible for her to sleep :
most often she could not remain in her bed, or
in any single place, incessantly going from one
to another. When she saw the day dawning she
rejoiced, thinking it would be that one in which
her desire would be satisfied : if night approached,
it was her idea, that the obscurity and isolation

from creatures must enable her to find that which she ardently longed for. In short, she was so transported out of herself and so smitten with the desire of uniting herself with her Beloved, that she often told me, speaking of this time, that " if any one had assured her she would have found him in the depth of the sea, she would have eagerly cast herself into it ; that if she had seen Hell opened with all its torments and had believed, she would have found in its depth him who had wounded her heart she would have hurled herself therein more quickly than the stone flies to its centre, and that all the pains of that place would have been agreeable to her, provided they aided her to enjoy her Love."

There came upon her at this time a violent desire to die. Her greatest pleasure was to think of Death as the sole means of attaining her aims. When she heard the knell for a dead person, or learned that some one had deceased, she felt a great joy and used to say to herself, " O would to God that I was in the place of this person, to see the object of my Love." The Devil, who never sleeps, and uses every opportunity to surprise the friends of God, made use of this great desire for death to tempt her to kill herself, in order the sooner to enjoy God. Once when she was on the margin of a pond, thinking what she could do to find her only love, she heard a voice which said inside of her, "Cast thyself into this pond and death will fulfil thy desire," and at the same moment she felt as if a push to make her fall in ; but a fear of offending God restrained her, otherwise she would have cheerfully cast herself in. Wherever she was, or however engaged, she was always occupied in her interior, thinking of the Object of her Love and the means of enjoying him, and she felt such extreme pain at seeing herself so long deprived that oftentimes she said to God, " My Lord, take away my life, or tell me where I shall find you, for I cannot live without you." Other times she called him by all the names most likely to incite him to unveil himself, which love could suggest, " O my God, how infinitely amiable you must be, since not knowing you and not knowing who you are, I am dying and languishing for love of you ! "

Sometimes she was seized with a holy and loving impatience, and called him cruel and pitiless to keep so long hidden. She said to him " You do indeed make yourself to be sought for, Love, and make me run after you ; but if once I am able to find you, O never, never will I let you go."

Other times she thought of herself as a poor straying sheep who had lost its shepherd and was doing all it could to return to the fold of Jesus Christ, and she said to him, " O good Jesus ! you are the good shepherd who runs incessantly after sheep that flee from you ; and I who so long seek you, from me you still keep fleeing. What do you want me to do, and to whom shall I have recourse ? Make me to hear your voice, and bring me into your flock, and place me in your company, that I may never be separated from you." Love made her utter all these words with a tenderness and feeling that cannot be told, and made her play all sorts of parts and use all means she could think of as likely to aid her in attaining her aims.

Not only did she address our Lord, but also all the Saints male and female who were connected with his sacred Humanity. But being divinely instructed and knowing well that the most powerful means of attracting God and obliging him to unite and unveil himself to her, was the solid practice of virtues, she gave herself to it with all her strength, and never let pass an opportunity of enduring, of humiliating herself, of obeying and of conquering herself in everything, which she did not eagerly embrace. In so doing she had no other motive than to bend and incline the

c

divine mercy to have pity and compassion on
her poor heart ; which languished and pined
away in waiting the accomplishment of her desire,
that had reached such a point, she knew not
which side to turn to.

CHAPTER V

AFTER this faithful Spouse had, through the ardour of her desire, knocked and beaten at the door of Divine Clemency, at last it pleased his Majesty to fulfil the promise he had made, that " whoever seeks shall find, that it shall be given to him who asks, and that it will be opened for him who knocks." So he acted in the case of this his Elected, quenching the excessive thirst that he himself had kindled in her heart.

She had been for a long time in the state just described, and as the stone, when it approaches its centre, rushes with the greater impetuosity ; so the nearer she approached the term which God had destined for manifesting himself to her, the more her ardour increased. Accordingly from the commencement of Lent until Holy Week she found herself so excessively exercised by this desire to unite herself to the object of her love, that all previously experienced was as nothing in comparison of what she then felt.

As this holy time drew near, God, willing to put the last and finishing touch to dispose her for the great graces he was preparing for her,

gave her such clear views and knowledge of her
own abjectness and nothingness, that she saw,
as it were, an infinite distance and strange re-
moteness between God and her, owing to the infinite perfections of the one and the extreme
defects of the other ; and these views kept her
in such abasement that she dared not lift her eyes
to Heaven, nor address her prayers to God, judging herself unworthy of being heard : " I considered myself," she said, " as a poor criminal
who desires to enter into friendship with his
Prince, and not having the boldness to present
himself before him seeks intercessors in order
to re-enter into favour and to bring about the
peace he earnestly desires. I did exactly the
same with regard to the Blessed, sometimes
addressing myself to the holy Virgin, other times
to the Saints, then to the Angels ; in short, to
all the celestial company, supplicating them and
conjuring all to be my mediators with our Lord,
to obtain from his goodness the accomplishment
of my desire, which the view of my nothingness
and my sins in no wise diminished ; on the contrary, the more miserable I found myself, the
more I wished to unite to him whom I knew to
be my ALL and my only GOD."

In this way I spent all the time of the Passion,
and on Good Friday I went to the Sermon, where

I was only a quarter of an hour, hearing tell of the torments of my Saviour, when my heart was so outraged and pierced with sorrow that I was obliged to leave, lest it should break in pieces, or at least make its feeling apparent by some action. I withdrew to the house, where there was no one. I shut myself up there, and at first commenced running from place to place and crying until out of breath, like a mad person. Then throwing myself on the ground, I cried, " Mercy, Lord, Mercy ! " I asked the help of all the Celestial Court and conjured all the Saints to aid me, and addressing myself to God I said to him with a fervour all a-flame, " O my Lord, and my God ; the day is come on which I must be wholly yours. Purify and wash me in your precious blood ; anoint my heart with the oil of your mercy. Pierce me through with the arrows of your holy Love. Make me among the number of your Disciples. Show yourself to me and unite me to you."

" In the intensity of these prayers and uttering these words which were dictated from within (for as for me I knew not what I was saying and did not understand the sense of these words, nor the mysteries they contained ; but I was as if forced to utter them, which I did with such impetuosity that each word was like a sharp arrow to pierce the heart of God). At the intensest moment, I say, of this prayer, I was in an instant carried to the highest storey of the house, without knowing how. I found myself there without thinking. When there, I threw myself on the ground, unable to keep up, such distress was I reduced to, and at the same instant God made to shine in the depth of my heart a ray of his divine light, by which he manifested himself to me and made me clearly know, that he, whom I so much had desired, entered and took complete possession of me.

"At the outset of this great favour, I found myself quite clothed in and surrounded by light, while a fear seized me, but lasting only a moment. For immediately my heart was reassured and so changed that I no longer knew myself, and I felt such a satisfaction of all desires that I knew not whether I was in Heaven or on Earth. For some time I remained motionless like a statue, unable to stir. Since then all the powers of my soul have continued so filled and satisfied, and the peace was so great in all sentiments, that I could not doubt that God had united and intimately joined me to him, as I had so ardently desired, and I believed this truth with a certainty more infallible than if I had seen it with my eyes ; for the light which was then communicated to me far surpassed all that sight could perceive."

But who could now declare the blessings and divine riches she then received ?   Certainly only the heart which felt them could speak of them. Then all her requests which so ardently she had made of God were fully granted ; for in the first place, she felt so abundantly the effects of the divine Mercy that it seemed to her all her sins had been pardoned, and she never after felt their weight and heaviness as previously.

Secondly, she knew herself washed interiorly and purified in the precious blood of our Lord and anointed with the Unction of divine Grace.

In the third place, she found herself that instant despoiled and freed from all attachments, habits and inclinations to evil, and delivered from the love of all creatures.

In the fourth place, her heart was so shattered by the love of God that it was her opinion she had been pierced through and through with many arrows, and in fact from that blessed moment her heart was continually ill and sensibly wounded by love, except for the two years she endured the strange trial to be presently narrated.

Finally, for the granting her last request God unveiled and manifested himself so clearly to her, making her know that he dwelt in the centre

of her soul, that never after had she to seek him
as absent or at a distance ; but she enjoyed him
as present within herself, where his presence
made itself so sensibly known that never after
did she lose the sight, except for the time above
noticed. And therefore, when afterwards she
came to consider how exactly God had granted
her the substance of her prayers, she melted away
in gratitude and used often to say to him, " O
my God, my Love, my All, how well you knew
how to make me ask what you yourself wished
to bestow ! for as to me, I knew not what I asked
you. Blessed be your holy name for ever."

All her requests having been thus granted,
and feeling herself inflamed with ardent love, as
soon as she had a little recovered, she prostrated
herself body and spirit at the feet of our Lord,
and there in the presence of the most holy Virgin
and all the Celestial Court, whom she believed
most assuredly present at this spectacle of love,
she vowed and concentrated herself entirely to
the service of his Divine Majesty, and made the
vow of perpetual chastity. This she always
preserved in saintliness and angelic purity, notwithstanding the great attacks and strange
accidents which afterwards opposed it.

Immediately after this blessed day, which she
called " her day of blessing and conversion,"

she fell ill and continued so for five or six months
with a continued fever, which proceeded from no
other cause than the excess of the fire of love,
that quite burned and consumed her, as well in-
wardly as outwardly. In a little time she became
so weak and feeble as hardly to be able to support herself; and this gave an opportunity for
the opposition and trials she received soon after
from the hands of her mistress. For our Lord,
who in a moment had enriched her with such
favours, was not willing she should in the future
be deprived of a still greater and more signal
grace, namely, to suffer for his love many pains
and toils; that thereby she might be made like
her Beloved.

CHAPTER VI

THE fever which rapidly reduced her to great weakness was used by God to cool the esteem and friendship with which she had hitherto been regarded by her mistress, who began to be worried at seeing her constantly ill, and persuaded herself that, idleness being the cause of this unknown ailment, the only remedy was in work. Moreover, she thought that all those ardours, which externally appeared, proceeded from injudicious devotions, and that if moderation was not observed, this woman would weaken her brain and become mad. She was confirmed in this notion by a person of piety, who, having come to visit the lady, met her worthy servant, and remarked that there was something extraordinary in her mind. She asked what was the matter. The other, very obedient and ingenuous, told her simply whence it came and the ardent love she felt within. But, God, who willed to exercise her virtue, permitted that this person, though of extraordinary probity and much esteemed in the locality, attached no credence to her words and thought them the vain imaginings and fancies

of an empty head. She told her mistress that
she should keep a good eye on that woman, make
her work incessantly, and forbid all devotions ;
otherwise in a little time she would become entirely mad, being already well on the way.

This was enough : no more was needed to confirm an idea this worthy Lady already entertained, and being wise and prudent she feared
the misfortune might happen in her home. She
commenced therefore to work her in every way,
as I have subsequently learned from her own
mouth. Many times she has jokingly said to me
that if Armelle was a Saint, she had largely contributed to it, having acted towards her as a
worthy and severe Mistress of Novices ; and that
if the Life was written, there should be mention
of her in it ; but she would have found it impossible not to treat her so. Thus we see that it
was a special leading of God for the sanctification
of this virtuous woman.

During the three or four years that the trial
lasted her worthy mistress, being persuaded that
work would help in withdrawing her from that
state, greatly increased it ; for besides the former
occupation of looking after the children, she im-
posed on her everything most fatiguing in the
house-work, and directed the other servant not
to spare her and to leave to her whatever was

laborious and coarse in the work ; so that from
morning to night she had neither respite nor rest,
and the fatigue of the work, joined with the
fever, weakened her so, that often she was ready
to drop from weakness and lassitude. But her
mistress attributed all this to vain imaginations.

Her first work in the morning was to go to the
well, which was at a distance from the town, and
to carry on her head big pails of water. This
caused unbearable pain to her, so that every step
she made it seemed her head was being opened,
and often she could hardly see her path ; but none
the less she had to proceed. This was one of her
severest trials. Therefore God did not allow it
to last long, for her fellow-servant, who greatly
pitied her sufferings, relieved her, going there
secretly herself. But as to sweeping, making
beds, cooking and the rest of the house-work,
which was heavy, she dared not avoid that, nor
ask for help, however much she felt the toil and
pain. The best of it was, that whatever she did,
nothing ever pleased her mistress. She always
found something to censure, and seized every
opportunity to find fault, without this poor maid
ever saying a word, or showing in her actions
any movement of impatience or vexation. This
her mistress, however, did not attribute to virtue,
but regarded as stupidity or natural dulness,

and therein found a new ground for further despising her.

Once when fever, added to continued work, had so prostrated her that she could not stand, she was obliged to lie down ; but it was not for long, for her mistress, after a sharp scolding, made her get up and work, reproaching her, that it was her madness and laziness made her think herself ill, in order to have her ease ; and thereupon she ordered her to carry manure on her head into the garden, which was close to the house. Her nature shuddered with horror at this command, from the fear she had of a load on her head, owing to the strange pains it occasioned ; but none the less she went without replying, any more than a poor lamb, and for two days was engaged in this work. It was the most painful she ever felt ; every time she put the load on her head it seemed to her that someone was driving into it as many thorns as there were hairs ; but thinking of the Crown of thorns of our Lord made her find her own easy and bearable.

This was not the only occasion where she was so treated. Hardly a day passed that something similar to the above did not occur. If at times she was found leaning against a bench, or in some corner of the room (which she only did at the last extremity), her mistress made her leave the room and sent her to work, and when there was no house-work she invented some new task rather than allow a moment's rest. When she did anything not according to her taste her mistress reproached her with want of intelligence, although God had given her a natural grace of doing everything cleverly and elegantly.

At the commencement she felt these reproaches, especially when strangers were present ; for although of low condition, she had a noble and generous heart, very susceptible to shame and confusion, not from a sentiment of vanity, but through natural self-respect. God allowed that, when there was most company, it was then her mistress indulged most in these truths, as she thought them ; and at this Armelle felt a great joy in her soul, even seeking such occasions in order to mortify herself the more.

Such patience and rare virtues could come only from a heart greatly strengthened by grace, as might also be easily seen from the way she used to speak of the above.

" It seemed to me that all I endured was nothing in comparison with the desire I had to suffer after the example of my Saviour, who continually offered himself to me as the model for my actions. For in every circumstance he

Armelle Nicolas 47

instructed me from within, exactly as a Master would have done with his Disciple : and I made myself so attentive to hear his voice, and so prompt to carry it out, that I paid no heed to what was done to me, keeping myself close and shut up within myself with my divine Love, whose presence I never lost. There I conversed with him familiarly, and I rejoiced to suffer something for his Love, supplicating him to give me in a high degree the virtue of patience, which he had practised all his life. Other times, when the trouble was greater, I swiftly fled away and hid myself in the wound of my Saviour, which was my place and house of refuge. When there retired and shut in I would have defied all Hell. Such force and courage did I receive, and all I suffered appeared to me no more than a straw beside a great fire."

. A thing which much helped her was, that the young lady of whom we have spoken, who singularly loved her and greatly compassionated her on the suffering caused by her mother, used from time to time, in order to console and strengthen her, read from the "Imitation of Jesus Christ "; and whenever she opened the book, she failed not to find the chapter treating on Patience and how we ought to imitate that of the Saviour. This the worthy maid listened to as if the book had been written only for her, and hence arose a great desire to suffer.

At last, after five or six months of fever, it pleased God to give her back good health, but not to deprive her of the merit of suffering. On the contrary, he increased it more and more, permitting, that her worthy mistress forbade her going to Mass except on Festivals and Sundays, and prohibited all practice of devotion, believing, as said before, that it tended to make her mad. But this worthy maid laughed to herself at her mistress's notion and said, " No ; no, I am not mad now that I have found my divine Love, and that I love him with all my heart. It was formerly when I sought my God outside me that I was truly mad and senseless." What gave her most pain was this forbidding her to go to church, to which she nevertheless cheerfully submitted ; for she regarded her mistress with no other eye than she would have Jesus Christ himself and therefore, she punctually obeyed in everything.

When she could speak to her Confessor, she declared to him with full confidence all that passed in her soul and the opportunities of suffering which God furnished ; not as complaining of her mistress, but only to give him a full acquaintance with her interior. It was in a spirit of gratitude she received all the ill-treatment inflicted on her, and when the Father once said that she could leave the place, she replied with her usual fervour, " What, my Father, would you counsel me to quit and fly the crosses God has sent me ? No, no ; I will never do it, if you do not absolutely command me, and though I should suffer a thousand times worse, I will not leave this house until I am put out by the shoulders." Her Confessor was fully satisfied and encouraged her to persevere.

She passed thus about four or five years in that house, of which the first year and a half were employed partly in the lively apprehensions of her Saviour with responsive feelings and deploring her sins, partly in strong and furious temptations, which the devils presented, and a part in desire and excessive thirst to unite herself to her Beloved, which at last she happily attained. The other three years rolled by in sickness, toil, fatigue, scorn, humiliation and rebuffs, described above and many others which I omit ; amidst all which she persevered, always uniform and content, in the practice of a high and heroic virtue.

D

CHAPTER VII

THE patience which this holy woman exhibited under all the contradictions that befell her was such that no one who knew it but was full of affection to her and edified ; more particularly in the house she lived in, where she was loved by all, with the exception of her mistress ; whose husband often reproved her and said she did ill in thus treating a poor maid that performed every kind of good service and whom he pitied. But she could neither see this nor conceive it, and she was surprised how any one could love her and approve what she did ; God so permitting for the greater good of his faithful servant, whom he willed by this means to purify and refine like gold in the crucible of suffering. After God had thus tried her for the space of about three years, he permitted that towards the end of the last year her worthy mistress recognized what had been apparent to all except herself. It happened in this way, as I learned from the mouth of that lady.

One day in Summer while they were in the country her mistress took a notion to bathe, and

having taken this worthy maid with her, on the
margin of the water, she perceived her in an
instant quite concentrated and shut up in herself, not uttering a word. At which chiding
she said to her, "Well, great stupid, what dost
thou dream of now?" As if waked out of a
profound sleep, she answered with great mild-
ness and simplicity, that she was thinking of
the extreme anguish and affliction which had
penetrated the heart of the Son of God as he
passed over the brook Cedron, which this water
had put her in mind of. She answered, "Who
told you that the Son of God passed over the
brook Cedron?" "I do not know," said she,
"but I am assured it was so"; and as she
spoke these words her countenance began to
flame up with great ardour and her eyes shed
tears in great abundance.

This so powerfully touched the heart of her
mistress, that from that time out changing her
opinion, she gradually recognized that she was
wrong in treating harshly so worthy a maid.
Her conduct formerly unbearable appeared to
her henceforth quite different ; her silence, her
gentleness, her patience, her submission, which
she had always attributed to madness or want
of intelligence, assumed other titles in her mind
and were recognized as true virtues, so that

commencing to love her and to trust her she
gave her full power in the household and permission to act as she thought fit, and was extremely troubled at having made her suffer so
much, although it seemed that she could not
have acted otherwise ; and in fact it was so.
She therefore often since said that God had
made her blind on this matter in order to aid
in the sanctification of that Soul. From that
time she greatly loved her and conceived a great
esteem for her virtue, and ever after continued
in that sentiment.

After God had accomplished the design for
which he had brought her into this house, and
she had acquired strong habits of virtue from
the contradictions she ' had there cheerfully
suffered, and everything began to be favourable
to her, he gave her the desire of leaving. The
Devil with all his artifices had not been able to
induce her at the time of her greatest persecu-
tions to take her discharge. Now that everything smiled she did all she could to obtain it.
But her mistress would not consent, and made
all possible offers to induce her to remain still
with her.

At this time the eldest daughter of the house
married a gentleman, who ordinarily resided
in the country in a house he had near Vannes.

When he wished to take his new wife there, the latter begged her mother to give her this worthy maid to take care of her house. She consented with regret to part with so faithful a servant, but the desire to gratify her daughter prevailed.

There remained only the consent of Armelle, which was obtained without difficulty, as she was very glad for many reasons, one of the principal of which was, that she saw herself by this means removed to a distance from her relatives, from her country, and her acquaintances. This she had long wished for, in order to be able to give herself more freely to the service and love of God, her only aim. Moreover, her relatives were constantly urging her to marriage, and she thought God had brought about this opportunity for her to escape their pursuits; besides, as she had a strong inclination to solitude, she persuaded herself that in the fields she would be in her element, and that nothing would hinder her being wholly God's and enjoying him at her ease. But the poor woman was much surprised to find it quite different from what she promised herself; yet all turned to her advantage, by ways far removed from her thoughts and unknown to all creatures.

CHAPTER VIII

BEFORE speaking of this trial through which God made her pass, it is well to describe her previous state, in order that turning from the one extreme to the other, we may more easily judge how rough and severe was the combat she had to endure. From that Good Friday, when our Lord communicated himself so abundantly to her, she hardly ever passed a day without enjoying his Divine Presence, which she felt sensibly and intimately in the depth of her heart. This caused so great a fire of love that often she knew not what to do to diminish its ardour. The great and vehement love kept her heart always in profound peace, and therefore she bore with sweetness and tranquillity all the vexations which befel her, and even relished them.

All the thoughts of her mind, the sentiments and actions of her will, and the aims of her heart, had no other principle, nor other end, than God, who was her Love and her Good ; so that in all her words and actions she had no design but to please God. Everything which did not tend to that was painful and disagreeable to her. Her greatest delight was to be alone in order to converse with God, who gave her great sweetness, tenderness, and consolations. It was very rare for her to experience dryness or aridity, and if God made her taste it sometimes it was only with the tip of the lips. Quickly the milk of consolation irrigated her heart, which through this means she found free and disengaged from affection and attachment to all creatures.

But when the poor woman found herself in the place where she expected to be most free, it was there she saw herself most bound and imprisoned in a strange manner; and where she proposed to herself to live in profound peace, it was there she encountered a terrible war, of which, if I dared, I would say God and the Devil were the authors: God to purify and sanctify her; the Devil to destroy and ruin her entirely.

Before this trial came upon her she had passed three or four years in the quiet and delights we have mentioned. I call *delights*, the time when she felt herself well with God as to the interior, and enjoyed his sweetness and consolations; and although she during this time suffered much from her mistress and as much as she could bear, these were but child's play and little tests that

God made of her constancy, in comparison with
what afterwards happened to her.

She said herself, " When the soul believes
herself well with God and experiences the effects
of his grace, all that can befall her, either from
the Devil or creatures, is mild and easy to bear ;
but when God withdraws and leaves her to herself, it is a strange wretchedness ; particularly
when she sees herself precipitated into such misfortune that she seems every moment to offend
God, without being able to save herself from it.
It is then truly a soul deserves compassion and
that she veritably suffers." She had good
ground for speaking thus, her experience rendering her wise in these matters. For she found
herself gradually abandoned and deserted by
God, without receiving any perceptible aid from
him. All her great fervours were dissipated,
and there remained with her not the least idea of
ever having had them ; nor any remembrance
of the graces and favours she had previously
received from God. All this was so erased from
her memory that for the space of two years not
a single notion of it occurred to her mind. Moreover, the desire and love of virtue was so weakened
that she did not seem to have ever had it.

But what is most deserving of compassion
at at the very time she found herself devoid

of the love of God, her heart was filled with an
infernal fire, her mind with filthy and abominable
thoughts, and the imagination occupied with the
most horrible representations that Hell could
suggest. I doubt not that God had given power
to the devils to possess, or at least to obsess her,
seeing the strange state she was reduced to for
two years. I do not delay to describe it in detail,
sufficient to say that everything the Devil could
invent to afflict a poor Soul in these matters
he practised upon her, who never gave the least
voluntary consent to those infamous suggestions.
It is not possible to tell the anguish and bitterness of this poor heart.

The mere idea she subsequently retained of it
was enough to make the hairs of her head stand
on end. Her mind was always plunged in great
sadness, which made her weep abundantly. No
memory of the graces and favours she had previously received remained. She only knew she had
made a vow of chastity ; but how or on what
occasion she had not the least notion. This
remembrance increased her pain, while she had
in her mind, as she thought, what was most
opposed to it. During two years never did a
thought, either of God, or for God, come to her,
which could afford the least sensible alleviation.
Her only good consisted in a fear of offending

God, which seemed graven in the very depth of her heart, and this fear never left her during the fight, and served as defence and bulwark to ward off the blows of the enemy.

In all the assaults he delivered he was unable ever to extract from her the least consent to the smallest imperfection, as she afterwards recognized. Often she has said so to me, with her eyes full of tears, quite melted and penetrated with love and gratitude to her divine Protector. However, this fear afforded her no consolation, for the more the fear of offending was imprinted on her heart, the greater was the pain she felt at seeing herself every day, as she thought, acting counter to it. At last God had reduced her to such extremity of misery that all things to increase and augment her torment were vividly represented ; all that could afford the least alleviation were erased from her mind.

Besides, during these two years, she had no one to whom she could confide and declare the deplorable state she found herself in ; and this was no small cross. For, as we have said, God had given her strong inclinations to allow herself to be guided by another's will and she had this truth deeply impressed on her mind, that if she acted otherwise, she would be lost. Therefore seeing herself deprived of that support under such deplorable circumstances, she was the more confirmed in the thought of her loss, of which she felt no doubt. This did not prevent her from using every effort to find some one to whom she could open her mind ; four times she came to Vannes for the purpose, to confer with some monk ; but God did not allow her to receive any relief. She had no settled Confessor and took the first of the Parish priests that offered. Very often she could not explain her state, or if she could, they did not understand it. However, they always encouraged her to be faithful and to hope for God's help, and they advised her to communicate every week or fortnight.

It is true that, seven or eight months before emerging from this painful state, she had an opportunity of speaking to her first Director, having been sent by her mistress to Ploermel for some days. She was exceedingly glad of the circumstance, and when she reached the town she went at once to see him and told him the miserable state to which she was reduced, and her desire to remain near him, and not to return to the place where she was deprived of assistance in her pressing needs. She begged him with tears to allow her to remain.

But this worthy Father, being enlightened by a special light, was in no way moved ; on the

contrary, penetrating the secret designs of divine
Providence for the guidance of this Soul, he gave
her an express command in the name of our
Lord, to return as soon as her business was
finished, and to encourage her he said, in a
spirit of prophecy, these words, " Go boldly, my
Daughter ; and do not fear that God is abandon-
ing you. No ; he will never do it ; and in whatever wretchedness you may find yourself, he will
still assist you ; the strain of the combat is not
yet finished ; but he will carry you through it
to your very great advantage." These words
were so efficacious that she submitted with
prompt obedience, though she felt great repugnance ; in spite of which she obeyed, since such
was the will of God. Doubtless this prompt
obedience helped her on the road to her complete
deliverance.

CHAPTER IX

WHEN the day which God had destined for the deliverance of his faithful servant was approaching, she was so excessively tormented with that infernal and disorderly love that it was beyond bounds and restraint. She had never experienced such strange pains as those which then agitated her, so that, seeing herself reduced to despair, all hope of remedy was taken from her mind; she no longer thought of it. Believing herself entirely abandoned of God and reprobate, she waited only for the hour when she should hear the sentence of her condemnation pronounced. But God had quite other designs. He permitted the Devil to use his interval, and to this effect that enemy one day delivered such a rough assault that she knew not what to do or where to turn.

It seemed to her that all the devils must carry her off, and the fire of unchaste love kindled so strongly that, not knowing where to cast herself, she left the house and went into the middle of a great plain to weep and lament her misfortune, without being heard or perceived by anyone.

Here are her own words : " When there, I cast
myself on the ground quite in despair ; and
transported out of myself, I began to groan and
lament my wretchedness in these terms. ' Alas,
miserable unfortunate that I am ! Why was I
born, to see myself reduced to such a great unhappiness ? Was it necessary for me to leave
my relatives and friends to come to see myself
burning and consumed with an infernal fire ?
Must my heart which is made only for God
have love only for the creature, and that, which
I have always so dreaded, befall me in such
strange fashion ? My God, take me from
this world that I may no longer offend
you ! ' Being in the depth of despair and
of my plaints God in an instant changed my
heart, so that from an extremity of pains I
found myself in an extremity of joy and of
contentment, without knowing how or by what
means.

" This was effected by such a marvellous exercise of God's power that one might attribute it
to a miracle, greater, it seems to me, than if God
had resuscitated my body from death to life ;
there took place so sudden and so great a
change that it cannot be described. In the
moment I found myself free and disengaged from
everything ; and it seemed that a heavy and

terrible load had been removed from off my
heart, and that the chains, which hitherto had
held me in such captivity, were entirely snapped
and broken for ever. Interiorly I found myself
in such liberty that I did not know myself. In
that instant I was shown the cares and kind-
nesses God had bestowed on me during my
misery; but with such distinctness and clearness that I was ready to die of love and gratitude,
and every time I think of this I know not which
is the greater miracle, whether my deliverance,
or the being able to support without dying the
excess of love my heart felt at that sight. It
was enough to have deprived me of life had not
God preserved me. I remained so weak for near
an hour I was without power to move or even
to breathe, stretched out as if dead. Through
the mercy of God I was so to all creatures, to
live no longer but to him, who henceforth took
such a possession of my soul, that never since
has he abandoned or deserted me for a single
moment."

When she had a little recovered, it is impossible to tell the thanks she gave our Lord.
She melted in tears, but they were tears of love
and sweetness, and the peace she felt was so
great that it far surpassed all the troubles she
had previously experienced; and she found

herself enriched with gifts and graces from
our Lord which cannot be declared. Among
others God gave her so living a *faith* and
such firm *trust* in his goodness, such ardent
charity, that, it seemed to her, nothing in
the world could separate her from her God;
and never after could the Devil, world, or
flesh, disturb her in the slightest in his
service.

There was further given such an *empire* over
herself that it seemed all passions had been
annihilated, particularly that of love. Never
after did she feel the least spark of affection for
any creature, save so far as God ordained it.
On this point she used to say at times, that
our Lord had healed her by the strangest
remedy — the very sentiment of disorderly
love of the creature; and that God had
given her the greatest good she could have
wished, through the greatest evil she could
have dreaded; and had made use of filth to
purify her, as in the case of the blind man
in the Gospel, where he used mud to give him
light.

After she had been about two hours giving
praise to our Lord, blessing him and thanking
him for all his mercies, calling upon the Holy
Virgin, all the Saints of Paradise and all

creatures, to aid her in praising him for all his goodness, and all the graces and favours he had just bestowed on her, she returned to the house, but very different from what she was when she left it.

CHAPTER X

ABOUT this time there arrived at Vannes a
Father of the Company of Jesus, well-known and
esteemed by the father of the young lady with
whom this worthy servant lived. On hearing
of his arrival the lady was advised by her father
to take this Father as her Confessor, and he gave
her a great account of his virtue and merits.
Armelle, hearing this discourse, determined to
apply to him and to open out to him fully the
state of her soul. But she did not dare of her
own accord to present herself to him, and knew
not how to find an opportunity of speaking.
Having affectionately recommended the matter
to God, praying, if it was his will, that he
would himself furnish the means of attaining her
end, she went to Vannes to the Jesuit College.
Meeting at once the gate-keeper with whom she
had some acquaintance, she asked him if some
Father would be willing to hear her confession.
This worthy Friar showed her a confessional,
and said, " Go to that Father ; you will certainly
find there the person you are looking for." He,
however, knew nothing of her design.

In truth he made no mistake ; the Father to
whom he directed her was the same of whom
she had heard speak. She went to him and
confessed, receiving much consolation, without
however daring to open herself for this time ;
but, on the second occasion when she returned
to confess, she asked him if he would allow her
to open freely the state of her soul. The Father
let her know he was quite willing, and appointed
a day so as to do it more conveniently. On
her side she did not fail to keep the appointment,
when she spoke to him and fully related her
dispositions both past and present ; but with
such clearness, humility, discretion, and prud-
ence, that this Father was quite charmed to hear
a poor village girl speak thus. He was astonished to see the treasures of Grace and virtue
shut up under that simple exterior, and from
that time he knew the high designs God had for
this maid, and felt a strong desire to aid her
in removing and destroying every hindrance to
divine Love which he could observe in her heart.

For this purpose he offered himself entirely to
her, to assist her in all her necessities, and enjoined her to have recourse to him with full confidence and at any hour, assuring her he would
always be ready to aid her to the utmost of his
power. This he henceforth did not fail to do,

under all circumstances. To begin, he wished
to know if there was not in her soul some imperfection, some attachment, some defeat, some
movement of selfhood, that he might direct
there his care and watchfulness, in order to up-
root and entirely remove all that was opposed
to God ; for the general conducting of this Father
tended always to an entire destruction and subjection of the passions, that the soul might be
left free for the operations God wished to effect
in her.

One cannot express the joy and consolation
the worthy woman received from having met
this Father, so full of zeal and charity for her
advancement : and on her side she promised
courageously to follow all his orders, entreating
with hot tears that he would not spare her in
anything he should see necessary, that God
might be absolutely Master of her heart, that he
should not regard her life, health, ease, honour,
satisfaction, or anything whatever. She said
this with such ardour and vehemence that she
seemed beside herself.

From the time she placed herself in his hands,
she was always so submissive and obedient, that
never did she depart one iota from whatever he
prescribed, and she would not have been willing
to do the least thing without his permission.

Although some years afterwards, by the advice
of this Father, she communicated with some
others of the same Company, who much aided
her, she nevertheless always continued, as far
as she could, to confess ordinarily to him, re-
cognising that she was indebted to him for the
great help he gave her at the commencement,
and the care he always took of her.

The acquaintance with this Father was extremely useful to her, not only for the care he
took to despoil her of the smallest imperfection,
and to make her practise the most solid virtues,
but for the assurance he gave her, that all, which
had passed and was passing in her, was from
God, and that they were the effects and certain
marks of the great love which he bore her ; as
before said, she always had been under some
sort of fear lest the Devil had insinuated himself among so many extraordinary things which
took place in her ; and that Carmelite, her first
Director, who had much assisted her, gave her
no assurance to the contrary. But the present
one made her clearly see that all proceeded
from the goodness of our Lord towards her ;
even the miserable state in which she had spent
her two years was an effect of his mercy, thereby
purifying her and rendering her capable of his
gifts. From the time her fears were removed,

one cannot describe how the ardour of her
love to God was increased. Therefore she used
commonly to say these words to our Lord, " O
my Love and my All ! it seems that nothing is
to deprive me of life but your Love alone and
the knowledge of the goods I have received
from your bounty."

CHAPTER XI

A LITTLE time after this holy woman had been thus withdrawn from the miserable servitude, wherein we have seen her, divine Love through the favour of God seized powerfully upon her heart in the following manner. One day considering the love God had exhibited to her on so many occasions, and desiring to respond to such an ardent Love, she felt herself on fire and quite moved within, and commenced in great fervour to ask our Lord that he would shatter and wound her heart with his divine Love. In the height of her prayer she perceived her heart sensibly transpierced, as if split and pierced from every side by arrows, but with a pain so great and excessive that she knew not what to do ; and from that time, during many years, she was not a moment without feeling a keen and strong pain in the heart, at one time, in one fashion, at another, in another, according to the disposal of God.

But for the first two years after this grace, the pain she felt was quick and ardent, of a force and vehemence so great that she seemed to have a fire within which was destroying and entirely consuming her. So that she was compelled to do extraordinary things, like a mad person. Though externally she appeared to suffer much, yet within herself she enjoyed so profound a peace, and her consolation was so great that she seemed to have all the joys of Paradise enclosed in her heart.

During these two years she shed abundance of tears : one saw her continually with tears in her eyes. She used often to say to her Confessor, when he was astonished at seeing her weep so, " My Father, though I should shed as many tears as there are drops of water in the sea, my love and gratitude for the goodness of our Lord would not be yet satisfied." What is worthy of note is, that, notwithstanding such continual weeping, she never felt any pain in the head. It was always the heart which was affected and whence originated the extraordinary effects apparent in her.

That fire which had been kindled in her heart extended itself, sometime after, throughout her whole body, so that one could not touch it without perceiving an extreme warmth. This caused a strong fever, which lasted for eight months, during which she was almost always in bed, her weakness being so great she could not stand.

It was then God made known the treasures of
graces and virtues he had enclosed in this blessed
soul. One cannot tell how she suffered, nor
the joy and content with which she bore the
pains, the scorn, the desertion and the neglect
of the servants. Often she passed whole days
in the height of her illness without being assisted
or tended by any of them. But on the other
hand, her divine Spouse did not forget her;
the more abandoned by creatures the more was
she caressed by him, which made her ardently
wish a still greater neglect, in order that being
deserted and deprived of all assistance, she might
put all her trust in him alone.

But God, who never abandons his own, and
who takes the more care of them in proportion
as they abandon themselves, did not fail to
succour his faithful servant through means of
her Confessor, who, knowing of her great sufferings, and the need of treatment, more easily
procurable in the town than in the country,
induced her mistress to have her brought to the
house of a virtuous widow for treatment. There
he took great care of her and called in Physicians
who prescribed for her; but the illness being
beyond their scope, the remedies were without
effect.

Her Director made her known to two other

Fathers of the same Company, one of whom
was Father Jean Rigoleuc, whose memory is
held in reverence by all who knew him ; the
other, Father Huby—two persons very zealous
for the glory of God and the perfection of
souls and very enlightened in the conducting of
spiritual persons. One cannot tell the cares and
attention these Fathers bestowed on her and the
love they bore her, seeing in her the true effects
of a sincere and perfect love to God. They
found particular consolation in talking with her,
for all the discourses were so many sparks of the
sacred fire which burnt her heart, and she had
no greater pleasure on her part than in simply
declaring to them all God was operating in her.
This she did in terms so humble, so burning,
so holy, that it was quite apparent God was
speaking in her rather than she herself.

It was a wonderful thing to see and hear this
blessed creature, for all her discourse was only
of God and of his divine Love. She resembled
a Phœnix expiring on his pyre, or better, a soul
truly seraphic, which had neither life nor movement save to love and to die in loving. These
Fathers endeavoured to moderate a little this
great ardour, advising her not to allow herself
to be carried away to the great excesses she felt ;
but it was not in her power to resist, for it seemed

she must die if she did not thus love. She told them that love alone was the cause of her life, as well as of her illness, and that as well the little strength she had proceeded from her love, as her illness.

CHAPTER XII

SHE passed thus eight months, always in bed, and with a fever which gave her no respite, so that her Confessor, seeing her illness continue, thought right to cause her to return to the country, hoping the change of air might give some relief. Accordingly, after being there some time, she began to improve, and sometimes got up, until she found sufficient strength to occupy herself in house-work; for as she has told me herself, love so transported her then, that as soon as she had the least good health, she worked indefatigably, and would have liked to do by herself the whole work of the house, urged to it by her interior instinct. Thus she passed the three or four years after being delivered from the state of temptations of which we have spoken, both before and after that fever of eight months.

At this time it happened that we needed a Sister lodge-keeper, having only one, who was insufficient for the services of the House; and we turned to the Confessor of this worthy maid to have one from his hand, as we had great con-

fidence in the Father. On his part, having
great affection for our Community, he thought
he could not better satisfy us than in giving
us this virtuous woman. It was easy to find an
opportunity for taking her away from the large
household where she was, because he saw that
her continual occupations were a great obstacle
to her recovering her strength and former health.
For a long time he had been looking out for an
opportunity of procuring her some relief. God
gave him one quite suitable in this circumstance, to our great satisfaction; for we had
heard much of the virtue of this worthy woman,
and were very glad to have her in our House.
But her master and mistress would not consent.
They exceedingly felt her leaving, and loudly
complained to the Father, and showed their
resentment the whole time of her absence. As
to the worthy Armelle, she had no difficulty in
doing what was commanded her, and thus she
left the place where she had sustained such
rude combats and where God had loaded her
with such graces.

While in our House, she began gradually to
recover strength, not that she attained perfect
health, but she was much better than she had
been for a long time. We had a singular friendship for her, and we endeavoured to give her

every possible relief, not allowing her to work at anything which could affect her health. Besides, she was with a worthy woman who had long been in the service of our Community as lodge-keeper, and who tenderly loved her and would not allow her to suffer the least inconvenience, preferring to go all our messages herself rather than let her do any work which might fatigue her too much. Thus she led an easy life. She behaved with such virtue, silence, modesty and submission that all the nuns who had business with her were extremely edified.

Many often asked permission to go and talk with her, and it was their great pleasure to hear her talk of God and his holy Love, particularly on the days she had communicated. One seemed to see and hear a second St Catherine of Sienna, or of Genoa, so ardent and full of fire was her discourse ; but to enjoy it one needed to proceed cautiously and oblige her to speak as if without thinking ; otherwise she never would have done it. Her humility and respect for the nuns was so great that she was always silent in their presence. When, however, Love carried her away, or she was led to treat on this subject, then she said marvels, and it was clearly the heart was speaking through the mouth.

She spent a year and a half in this state, very happy, and recovered her health to a great degree. It seemed this was God's purpose in bringing her. Then she commenced to hold in horror and disgust all the ease and convenience she here received, her interior instinct having always inclined her to what was hard and displeasing to nature. The more she was loved and cherished, the more her pain. It was intolerable to her spirit to see herself happy and at ease, though nature greatly enjoyed this state ; for to see that she suffered nothing was to her a great affliction.

This caused her to desire ardently to return to her former place ; but to speak of it was out of the question, and she saw no prospect of carrying out the design. Neither her Confessor nor the nuns would ever have consented. So far from it, they wished to receive her as a Sister after she had served some years. With this object they made her enter the enclosure of our House, that she might help in the house-keeping for the Boarders.

She was employed in serving the Boarders, of which she acquitted herself with so much gentleness and care, that all the little girls loved her and had such trust in her that she was their refuge ; and they bore her such respect, though

a servant, that they feared more to displease
her than their mistresses. Her presence alone,
and the modesty which appeared in her
countenance, was more than enough to keep
them to their duty.

She was careful that nothing should be wanting
in their service, and she did everything with such
order and tranquillity, that one would not think
she had anything to do. Her devotions were
so regulated that they offered no obstacle to
the discharge of her work. Often when she
was in the middle of her work there came upon
her such violent assaults of the divine Love that
she knew not what to do ; yet she continued,
and God provided relief. I was then engaged
in the instruction of the Boarders, and as soon
as I perceived her disposition, I used to send
her to rest quietly in some retired place. This
was the greatest relief one could offer her, and
as soon as there was anything for her to do,
immediately she returned to her work as if
nothing had happened.

During the whole time she remained in our
House never did anyone observe in her a word
or action showing the least defect ; on the contrary, genuine and solid virtues were there so
evident that they gained the love and esteem
of all who knew her ; which secured her against

any trouble or contrariety on their part. But
this state was too soft for her; God was not
willing she should long enjoy it; therefore he
soon withdrew her, using the means to be told
in the following chapter.

CHAPTER XIII

WE have already remarked, that for some time back this maid felt herself troubled and straitened notwithstanding the rest and contentment she received in our House, being conscious of a certain movement that made her know it was not the place God wished her to be in. None the less, she used every effort to free herself from this thought, being persuaded that nowhere could she be better off than in this House, where the examples of virtue were constantly before her. Besides, the affection we had for her and the good will she recognized in our Mothers to keep her for the remainder of her days, in addition to the wish of her Confessor that she should remain there—all these reasons were powerful motives to induce her to remain in a place every way so advantageous.

But God, who does not wish that Souls he desires to be wholly his, should regard their own interest in opposition to his will, finally made her see clearly that it was his will she should leave this House, where according to all appearance she could want for nothing, and where her inclinations had received much satisfaction. For this purpose then he allowed her to commence to feel in a marked manner the vivacity of her passions, which hitherto had been as if entirely deadened; moreover, nature was much more than ordinarily disposed to gratify its appetites, and although she did not indulge, but on the contrary nobly repulsed them; nevertheless, she was troubled to find herself engaged with an enemy, who long before had laid down his arms and appeared conquered.

But what astonished her most was, that she recognized a change in her interior state; for that great and continued familiarity, which she had always enjoyed with our Lord, and the extreme love that possessed her began to grow dull; not that she for this failed in being as faithful as before; but there was more of fear and restraint, and a certain contraction of the heart she had not been in the habit of feeling. This made her begin to think seriously of the means of obeying the movements she had up to then concealed.

And what urged her still more to this, was an occurrence which happened a short time before leaving. One night, being between awake and asleep, she seemed to be on the edge of a precipice, over which she was just about to fall; and being

greatly alarmed and in trouble, not knowing
how to save herself, two persons clothed in black
presented themselves to her, who gave her their
hands and drew her back from it. On this she
awoke, her mind full of fear and of confidence
at the same time. It was beyond her power to
drive away the idea of this dream, whatever her
efforts, although she did not understand what it
pointed to.

But she was not long before she learned : I
think it was next day, or certainly a few days
after, a monk of the order of St Dominic, a near
relative, came to see her, and severely repri-
manded her for having left her first dwelling,
saying among other things these words, which
touched her keenly : " Is it thus," said he,
" that you love the Cross and suffering ? You
fly them to come and seek your ease in a place
where nothing vexes you. What will you answer
our Lord when he will reproach you, that, in
spite of the movements he gives you for a life of
greater suffering and contempt, you still persist
in following your human, natural reasonings ? "
Then, continuing his discourse, he added : " I
tell you in the name of God that you are here
against his will, and that he calls you to the
Cross, not to rest."

These last words made a strange impression

on her mind, which was increased by a circumstance, worthy of remark, namely, that she had
not in any way made known to this worthy
Father the state of her soul, nor said the least
word that could lead him to make these con-
jectures ; on the contrary, although he declared
so openly what was passing in her on the subject
of her leaving, she gave him no information as
to her movements thereto ; only she was much
moved and began to weep. He continued
strongly urging her to leave, for no other reason
than that he was incited thereto by a secret
guidance of Divine Providence, who made use
of him to announce his will to that Soul. Accordingly, she received his discourse in no other
sense ; for it was too manifest that, without a
special knowledge from God, this Father would
not have spoken to her in these terms ; and it
seems that he had come into the neighbourhood
for this object alone, as he left immediately.
Many years had passed since he had seen his
worthy relative, and he left her much afflicted,
resolved however to obey the will of God, so
manifestly declared unto her.

She saw already one part of her dream come
to pass ; those persons clothed in black who
gave their hands to her being none other than
this monk and Father Rigoleuc of the Company

óf Jesus, whom we have already mentioned, to
whom she declared fully the state of her soul.
This worthy Father had been absent from the
locality from the time of her entering our House,
and, on his return, which was at the time her
mind was agitated, both by the interior movements and the words which her relative had
said to her, he found this poor woman in much
trouble.

She fully declared to him how everything
had passed, the unwillingness and opposition she
had felt at her coming to us, the strong and
violent movements towards leaving in order to
be able to suffer and endure more, the dream
she had had, and then the conversation with
that monk ; but particularly the cravings of
nature, the rebellion and agitation of the passions
and the coolness she felt on the part of
our Lord ;—all this, I say, she declared with
great simplicity and openness to this worthy
Father.   He, judging from her recital, and
particularly from the change in her interior
state, that undoubtedly God wished her elsewhere, since he gave, such clear indications,
after having recommended the business to our
Lord and seriously thought thereon, gave her
for answer, that he gave her an order in the name
of the Holy Spirit to return to her former

dwelling-place. These words were uttered with such power and authority that they made a powerful impression in her heart, receiving them as from God's own mouth. Henceforth, therefore, she thought of nothing but the means of executing them, and all her difficulties disappeared.

God, who was conducting this business, was not long in providing for her a means exactly suited; for the lady with whom she had lived had never ceased since her departure in trying all possible means to get her back again; but up to this, always unsuccessfully. Now being pregnant and exceedingly ill, she greatly feared some mishap in her confinement, and speaking in this sense one day to the Father, with whom she was well acquainted, she said to him, that if only she could have her Armelle near under these circumstances, it would be a great consolation to her. The Father, seizing the opportunity, told her to ask her from our Mother Superior and that he did not think she would be refused in such a just request. The lady, well pleased with the assurance, immediately went to see our Mother Superior and asked for her with such urgency that she was granted to her, with the expectation of her subsequent return.

But God disposed it quite otherwise; for

once she had her in the house, the lady would
never consent afterwards that she should leave
it ; and besides, this maid urged nothing to the
contrary, proofs of God's will being too evident
for her to oppose it.

Her Confessor and our Mothers often begged
her to return, and the love she had for the House
and the desire to serve it were powerful motives
to make her incline to do so ; but the will of
him to whom her whole life has been submitted
incomparably outweighed everything. At this
time and a little before she left us, her mind was
keenly impressed by the words that Jesuit Father,
whom we have mentioned and of whom we
will speak much in the course of this narrative,
had said to her, when he left Vannes for three
of four years, which was about the time this
worthy woman was in our House ; this Father,
I say, in whom she had perfect confidence, when
bidding her adieu, said to her only these few
words, which were like future presages of the
state she found herself in a little after, " My
Daughter," he said, " I have only one thing to
recommend you, that is, that you remain firm
and immovable as a rock in the midst of the
sea, which, though beaten by waves and attacked
by the winds, does not stir or incline to one side
or the other : so when it shall happen to you to

be pushed and agitated by diverse movements,
and those who conduct you have different advice
for you, look at that which is most conformable
to the will of God and attach yourself strongly
to it, without giving yourself any trouble except
to follow it, let what will happen." This was
the farewell the worthy Father gave her at his
departure, and it so strongly recurred to her
mind in the matter of which we are speaking
that it seemed to her to have been said merely
to strengthen her in this conjuncture ; for previously she had not at all reflected on it, but
on the present occasion it was so impressed
within her, that nothing in the world could have
shaken her.

In fact, it was regard to God alone, which,
against the sentiments of those who wished her
well and her own natural instincts, enabled her
to take the step ; for with exception of those
two Fathers, her relative, the Dominican and
Father Rigoleuc, all who knew it were opposed
to her leaving us : those two, as she had seen
in her dream, lent her the hand to withdraw
her from a place which could not be hurtful,
save because God wanted her elsewhere ; for
otherwise it would have been to her a Paradise
of delight. But as the perfection of exalted
Souls, such as hers, consists only in the perfect

accomplishment of the will of God, it is a martyrdom to them in the slightest degree to fall short,
and they cannot be at rest until they entirely give
themselves up to it.

The love she always preserved and the esteem
she had for this place were proofs sufficient to
let us judge the motive of her leaving, which was
solely as we have already stated. She left it
as to her corporal presence, but her heart was
bound by strong and holy bonds. It was the
usual place for her visits, and here she came from
time to time to give outlet to her flames and fan
that divine fire which devoured her entrails, in
the intimate conversation she used to hold with
some of this House.

All our nuns also on their side preserved a
great love for her, owing to the esteem they had
for her virtue, and all deemed themselves happy
to have a share in her prayers : many with great
confidence recommended to her what they wished
to obtain from our Lord, and ordinarily not
without success. Not only did she pray for our
nuns individually but also for the entire Community, and often through a spirit of gratitude
she used to say, she would never in this world
or the other forget the blessings she had received
here ; sometimes she called it her house and
place of refuge ; because, said she, it is the house

of my father, God ; and children trust themselves in what belongs to their father. It was
the great confidence she had in the goodness
of our Lord which made her speak thus. At
last, seeing that during her life she could not
dwell here, she asked, with great humility, and
for the love of our Lord, from our Mother
Superior, that after her death she might be
buried in some little corner of our chapel. This
was very willingly granted by our Mother and
our Community.

CHAPTER XIV

As all the life of this blessed woman was nothing else but a life of love, it is impossible to speak of any part without speaking of this same love. Therefore this and the following chapters will be almost full of it, certain though we are that all we shall say, or that could be said, on the subject, will prove but as shadow to substance and be only a part of the truth. Passing on then from what has already been written and her experiences previous to the severe trial of the two years, I will particularly set out the order God observed in his subsequent leading; whence may be easily gathered the loving care his paternal goodness had to draw her to the highest stage of perfection by the road of his divine Love.

Having in the first instance, for a space of two years, left her in wretchedness and affliction and quite extraordinary privation, as well on his part as on that of all creatures, as narrated in the eighth chapter, for recompense he willed that the following three or four years should pass in a very vehement and ardent love. This

love at its commencement was mingled with
so much regret and bitterness, at seeing that
her heart had been occupied by any love but
that for her God, that it sometimes seemed to
her that it was breaking in pieces, a thing which
took place not by thought or imagination ;
but she actually experienced a pain more penetrating than if one had cut it in pieces. During
this time she was continually moaning, and saying
things so penetrating and conformable to the
sentiment of her heart, that it was impossible
to hear anything more touching. Her regrets
were accompanied with such floods of tears that
day and night her eye was scarcely ever dry.

Love and regret were then so united and mixed
together, that she knew not which of the two
occupied it most. And in truth it was not love
alone which caused these effects, that one may
properly call the effects of painful love, which
she felt for about a year. Afterwards all these
regrets and bitternesses were taken away from
mind and heart ; she passed on to a second
state that effaced from her memory the sight
and idea of her abjectness, to leave her only the
remembrance of the great mercies God had
shown her. Thence followed a love so great,
that she fell ill from it and seemed about to die,
as we have already said, when she felt continu-

ally her heart inflamed, and penetrated by a sharp dart which caused desires, and gave her strength to work for God, that is beyond belief, and did not rest in mere desires, but passed on to genuine effects. Nothing appeared to her troublesome or difficult, the vehemence of this interior spirit which animated her making her devour everything, when the question was of working for God; and this was constantly occurring, for it was the motive of all her actions. She was pushed to it with such an interior impetuosity that she seemed rather to fly than to walk. All that was most onerous was what she seized upon with the greatest ardour, and never was she more satisfied, nor more happy in what she did, than when she toiled; for the more she endured, the more insatiable of troubles and suffering was she.

It was not merely in external matters that she was thus energetic and unwearied, This same love which occupied her exteriorly led her also in a different way from within; where the continual presence of God kept her in perpetual movements to testify her love to him; and this she did in a thousand ways; sometimes she adored and thanked him for his benefits, offered herself and consecrated herself to his services; sometimes she praised him and invited all

creation to bless him; at other times she humbled
herself and sunk herself in the knowledge of his
greatness and her nothingness; sometimes she
was led to exalt and magnify his divine perfections; but her most ordinary conversation
was of love, and this she carried on in all
imaginable ways.

There she lost herself, immersed herself and
was reduced to such extremity that she almost
fell into faints; but this powerful and impetuous love came to her help and straightway
strengthened her, and made her act as before
with such persistence, that she has often assured
me, not a moment passed during these times
without her working and being active in relation
to God. Even at night her rest was interrupted
almost every moment by these interior vehe-
mences, that woke her with such impetuosity,
that she knew not what to do to satisfy these
great transports.

All this was given to her without her procure-
ment, or doing the least action to carry herself
towards God. She did all she could to receive
what was given her by his divine Majesty, who
poured his graces into this blessed creature with
such abundance, as she said herself, that it
seemed a torrent or a deluge which engulfed
her; she was so filled that she overflowed, and

if she had not found some person to confide in,
she could not have borne them. When she had
no one she had recourse to the woods and to the
trees, or to other creatures, relieving herself by
calling upon them to bless, in their fashion, her
Beloved, and speaking to them of his divine
perfections, as if they were endowed with reason.
After that a deluge of tears relieved her and
saved the vessel of her heart from bursting under
the force of that new wine, which her divine
Spouse poured into it with such abundance.

It was also during this time that she seemed
to be always in a hot and burning furnace,
which inflamed her and utterly consumed her
body and heart, and which, so to say, devoured
her. " Yes," she said to her Director, " I am in
a furnace, but a thousand times more glowing
than any in this world, which seem to me but
cold in comparison with what I feel in myself."
In proof of which she added, that during the
greatest heat of summer, her duty as a servant -
obliging her to be generally before a great fire,
she no way felt its heat, and she would not know
she was near it but for seeing it with her eyes.
.From this one may judge of the interior ardour.
adored when, she sometimes said to me that God
herself and consel her prayers, for more than a
sometimes she prakad asked him very fervently

at the commencement, when he drew her to his
divine service, that he would remove and consume in her all that was displeasing to the eyes
of his adorable Majesty. " Not Lord," she used
to say, " by cutting, or tearing away, or destroying, but by burning and devouring everything with the fire of your holy love." She
added that she was quite powerless not to make
this request, though she did not well know what
she was asking : but when she had experienced its
effects, she could not sufficiently thank her divine
Love, and she said to me in a tone of admiration, " See, see, if he has not entirely granted me
what he made me ask for with such urgency ! "
It was enough, no more was needed to set her
entirely on fire, and deprive her of speech. Thus
was she ordinarily whenever she spoke of, or
remembered, the mercies of God on her behalf.
She used often also say to him in loving com-
plaint : " My Lord and my All, your love and
your bounties will make me die."

God having for a long time maintained her in
this state of Love, which one might designate
violent, strong, energetic, unwearied love, and
having by his efforts deadened and weakened
the vigour of her natural forces, of which he had
made much use in these violent operations of
his—he made her pass into another disposition

G

quite contrary to the former ; for her nature
having hardly any more vigour, she ˙fell into
such weakness and languor that she could with
difficulty support herself. The love she then
felt was far more quick and penetrating, but
being more remote from the operation of the
senses, it caused her far more weakness than
previously ; so that her life was only a continual
languor. Love still pursuing his conquests,
reduced her to such a state that she knew not
what would become of her.

She pined away to see God so little loved and
so little served by his creatures, and that he was
so little known, and that Souls he had pur-
chased with his precious blood, had other loves
and other thoughts than for advancing the glory
of her Beloved. The interests of his Majesty
touched her so powerfully, that she would have
despised all the torments of this world and even
of Hell to maintain them. These sentiments
in such a way filled her mind that nothing in
the world could divert her from them. She was
so consumed with this desire to glorify her God
that she hardly lived ; she perpetually sought
new means of increasing his glory, and this desire
so gnawed her, that often she said to me, that
there was no death, however cruel, that would
not be more tolerable to her, than what she felt

at seeing God forgotten and despised by his creatures. Sometimes she cried out, "Oh, if at least I was in a state to make known, and to be able to declare what I feel! No heart, were it of marble, but must break and give its love to him who has so loved it."

What she desired for others she admirably practised herself, for knowing that the most noble and excellent way of glorifying God is to love him, she acquitted herself of it with all her strength, and, as already said, her natural forces being all consumed, she borrowed from love itself strength and vigour to love more ; and when she found herself deprived of it, she was in such weakness that it seemed she must surely die. It was then she made these loving plaints to our Lord. " My Love and my All, I can do no more. I languish and die of love." This was what she used ordinarily say within herself at this period, and often out aloud without thinking, " No, I can do no more, I languish and die from excess of my love."

Her exterior appeared so languishing and broken down, that one would have pronounced her ill. She was so in fact ; but it was of no natural illness, for her constitution was perfectly sound, and her body well knit. Her ailments were always the effects of her love, and as it

operated within, the body externally felt the
effects, being during this period in an extreme
weakness; which however did not prevent her
from acting and discharging all her duties, as if
she had the strength of former days. Of these
things I can give a true testimony as I often
saw her in the house so broken down and
weakened after these violent assaults of love,
that I hardly thought she could move about for
two days to come; yet when the hour of work
arrived, she set herself to her task with as much
vigour as if nothing had occurred. I will give
one example out of many that I might adduce,
which deserves consideration from the loving
circumstances which accompanied it.

One night while this worthy maid was in our
house she was waked at midnight with great
vehemence, and at the same instant a strong
and violent love seized her, accompanied by a
presence of God so inward and essential, if one
may say so, that this poor woman knew not
what to do, nor where to go. She got up and
fell on her knees beside her bed, waiting for day
to go before the holy Sacrament. To tell what
passed within her then is beyond my power. At
last when day dawned she went to the choir,
thinking that there she would find some relaxation; but it was the very opposite, for her

heart warmed up still more at approaching the source of divine fire, which was already consuming her. Compelled to leave immediately, she went to the garden and took her Rosary, hoping by repeating it to escape from that powerful operation, which put her quite beside herself. But it was impossible to say a single *Ave Maria*.

That morning I went to the garden before rousing the community. I found this poor woman, who was at the limit of her strength, and from weakness let herself fall upon me. I took her into a neighbouring room the best way I could, and began questioning her as to the cause ; but it was more than a quarter of an hour before she could answer me ; at last coming back as if from a deep, self-concentration she said three or four broken words, which enabled me to judge sufficiently the state she was in.

When she had a little more recovered herself, she told me that since midnight God had carried on in her an operation, so powerful and violent, that she knew not how it was she was not dead, such was the excessive love ; and that the little strength she previously had had been taken away from her, God having wholly absorbed and swallowed her up in himself, so that she had less vigour than one on the point of expiring.

Saying this she began to weep, and thus relieved herself a little. But seeing her extremely weakened and that she had been without rest during all the night, I had her put to bed, believing it would be long before she could get up. I told her not to trouble herself about the service for the Boarders, but to take her rest, and then I went away.

When she found herself alone she commenced making such tender and loving plaints to our Lord that I cannot express. " Alas ! " said she, " my Lord and my God, what do you wish me to do in this world, since I cannot more love you ? Once you gave me strength to employ in your service, and now your love has consumed it all, and the little remaining to me you now come still further to annihilate ! What shall I do ? You know that my life is nothing else but your love, and how can I love you without strength and without vigour ? When I had strength it was all my joy and my delight to employ it for you. Ah ! what can I do now when I see myself deprived of it ? At least do you love yourself, O my Love, since I can no longer do it." She uttered these words with a heart so touched and so tender that it was capable of softening the hardest hearts.

I was engaged at prayers, and on my return

I was astonished to find her with the Boarders,
performing her house duties as if nothing had
happened, and surprised at such a sudden change
I asked her the cause of it. She told me with a
smile that he who had taken away her strength
was all powerful to restore it, when she had need
of it. From that out I was no longer astonished
at seeing her in these faintings, which were
so common with her that when she had no
occupation, Love surprised her powerfully, and
she lost all power of action ; but as soon as she
had to work, she did it with as much freedom
as if nothing had happened.

It seemed as if God only waited for her to be
at leisure to caress her and testify to her the
excess of his love. And when she was in her great
transport and excess of love if the time for performing any service arrived, it was clearly put
into her mind ; then she used to say with a confidence quite filial and loving, " My Lord, leave
me now that I may serve you in this particular,"
and at the same instant (wonderful goodness of
God !) he used to leave her, and she went to her
work. This often happened every day, chiefly
during the time she was in these loving languors,
which was for about eight or nine years.

Her mind during this time was always
occupied with God and in God, as in the first

four years, but in a different manner, for it was
not so divided as previously. For so many
different motives were not the principle, nor
the matter of her love ; but God alone, and the
desire of his glory, without regard to herself
or her interests, which she had so utterly forgotten that they seemed to have no existence.
Her interior occupation was stronger, more intimate, sweeter, more penetrating, and more
continuous than previously. But as God did
not will to leave her always in this disposition,
having designed her for a more perfect state, his
loving Providence conducted her to it by way
and means which will be noticed in the next
chapter.

CHAPTER XV

HER Beloved was not yet satisfied with having adorned and enriched her with so many graces. He wished to confer on her one, incomparably greater ; reducing her to a state, where he alone should be the author of all her actions. To accomplish this design his divine providence made use of two means, one exterior, the other interior.

The first was, to direct her for guidance to the Father of the Company of Jesus, whom, we have already said, she no sooner saw, than she recognised by an indefinable feeling as the person who would most aid her in reaching to perfection. This Father had great love and high esteem for this Soul, whom he saw to be extraordinarily favoured by the divine Majesty, and he accordingly gave her all the time and the leisure he could afford, in order that she might freely open out her heart to him, and by this means give some refreshment to that great fire which was consuming her.

This was the only relief and the greatest service one could procure her ; for, as to guidance, he

had only to listen and approve what God was
operating within herself, and which was leading
her to the greatest perfection one could have
desired. This Father listened to her quite at
leisure, and did not urge her in one direction or
the other. He neither pressed nor disquieted
her in any matter : only he led her to a total
and perfect surrender of herself, in order that
God might dispose of her according to his
adorable will ; and he endeavoured quite gently
to abate gradually those great and violent excesses of love, and to prevent her from yielding
to all their ardour, lest she should shorten her
days and have less time and leisure for being
perfected in the way of divine Love.

He also counselled her to take some little
diversion, by familiar conversation on the things
of God with some person in her confidence, to
give a little relaxation to her mind ; or else to
occupy herself quietly in something that would
withdraw her from a too great attention ; but
above all he urged her to act as simply as
possible within herself, without reflecting much
on her views or feelings. When she had un-
loaded her heart with her usual ardour, he used
to say to her quite gently, " Ah, well ! have
we not a good God, who well deserves to be
loved ? But you would not believe you loved

him enough unless you told him so, over and
over again, and you do not see, that he knows
and recognises our most secret thoughts, without
our telling him ; but your love would not be
satisfied unless you gratified it in this way."

At other times, when she spoke to him, he
said hardly anything and on her saying to him,
" My Father, you say nothing to me," he
answered, " My Daughter, when God speaks,
what can one say or do, except listen in silence
and calm ? " But she had difficulty in understanding how a soul could remain in silence,
and not testify the excess of her love. Therefore
he did not press the matter, but let her act
according to the movements of her spirit, contenting himself with gradually preparing her
for what he foresaw God willed to operate in her.

God, on his side, led her on the same road ;
for, as we have seen in the preceding chapter,
her great fervours and her reiterated acts were
moderated from a long time back, and her
languors and faintings had brought her into a
more peaceable and tranquil state, which every
day increased, particularly towards the close of
the ninth year of the period during which she
had been in these holy languors.

For hence she passed into a new state, finding
herself as if shut up and enclosed in the bosom

of divine Providence, which caused her such a
great interior calm, that she was, strictly speaking,
like an infant in the lap of its mother, who has
no other care but to allow itself to be carried
where ever she will. Exactly the same was she
in relation to God, all her desires and all her
aims having at this period no other object than
to leave her to the mercy of divine Providence,
that he might dispose of her according to his
good pleasure ; whence sprung a union so sweet
and so intimate with God, that she had never
experienced anything like it.

It was an excellent disposition for what God
was aiming at, and for which that Father prepared her, and this was the reason he strongly
incited her to abandon herself to God for ever,
and more, and more. Love, on its side, received
such accessions, that it extended incomparably
beyond her powers, so that it surmounted her,
and swallowed her up entirely. In consequence,
being unable to put bounds to it, or to restrain
her heart, she was often obliged to throw herself
on the ground or on a bed, and speaking to her
heart as to a thing she had no power over, she
used to say, as it were giving it up altogether,
" Oh, go, love as much as you will, for I am
unable to hinder or restrain you any more. You
are no longer mine ; you belong to Love alone."

All this served to advance her on the road of
God's designs, being much aided by another
disposition, which at this time she used to feel.
For after Holy Communion she no longer had
those sweet and loving colloquies, nor those
holy ardours, that used to kindle her ; but
instead she experienced a calm and a sweet
slumber in all her senses and all the interior
powers, as if strictly speaking she was resting
on the breast of the Son of God, like a second
St John. She was obliged to rest her head,
and often her whole body, on something to
support it, and would thus remain for up to
half an hour, unable to move or speak, unless
her household duties obliged her to withdraw.
In that case, she left everything to discharge
them ; otherwise, she remained thus, like a
person relieved and satiated, who having all that
he needs has nothing else to do or ask for.

While in these dispositions, enjoying the gentle
guidance of that Father, who approved strongly
what was passing in her, and to whom she addressed herself in all needs, it happened that he
received orders from his Provincial to go as Rector
to the College at Quimper, where Father Rigoleuc
already was, but who had come to Vannes some
days before on business he had there. The
worthy Armelle did not fail to see him and to

treat with him as with her Director, for they had both the same sentiments and the same affections for the conducting of her soul.

When she saw herself about to be deprived of both, and that she should remain without any aid or assistance, she was a little affected, but her feelings were soon calmed, regarding it as God's will to which she as perfectly resigned; as indeed she showed by her answer to these worthy Fathers. They counselled her not to be troubled at their departure, that God would not fail to provide her with what was necessary, either through their writings, or some other way. She replied, " My Father, in truth I feel your absence ; but if I knew you would love God better in the town where you are going than here, I would wish you already there, though I should never again see you." This answer greatly pleased them ; showing how God's interests prevailed with her over her own.

When the day of their departure came, her Director told her to communicate that morning. During the Mass she had much felt their removal, and whatever efforts she made to drive it from her thoughts, she could not succeed, God so permitting, to dispose her for the grace he wished to bestow on her. She gently complained to him and said, " Alas, my Lord, you are depriving me of my help and leaving me alone, without anyone

to whom I can speak and declare your adorable
wills ! What shall I do thus lonely, and to
whom shall I have recourse ?   Do you yourself be
my guide and my Conductor, since you deprive
me of those you had given me."

These words formed themselves in her mind ;
when she received the Holy Communion and had
the Host still in her mouth, our Lord said to her
interiorly and intelligibly these words, "My
Daughter, I deal with you as with children, who
are taken from the arms of their nurses to be
lodged in the house of their Father, that they
may receive there a better food than they
previously had : so with you, I wish to lodge you
in my house." Then she said to him, "Ah !
Lord ! where is your house ? " Our Lord
showing her the wound in his sacred side, made
her enter thereby into his heart, telling her, this
was his house. Lodged there, she found herself
in an immense void and great privation, so that
she did not see or recognise anything. This
made her say to him, "My Lord, you said here
was your house, I do not see or find anything at
all." No answer was given, but she experienced
a wonderful peace and repose.

After Mass the Father found this worthy maid
in the church, quite absorbed in God and so
loaded with the favours he had just bestowed on

her, that she knew not where she was, and was
as far as possible from troubling herself at his
departure. She told him shortly what had
happened, which greatly consoled this Father.
He charged her to declare to me all the state of
her soul, (so far at least as she should judge proper)
that from time to time I might communicate to
him what passed in her, and thus he might render
her the usual assistance. Thus he took leave
of her without her almost perceiving it, her mind
being in the situation just told.

When she had to do anything with attention,
she seemed to herself to come out from the heart
of Jesus through his sacred side as through a
door, and when she had finished her work, she
re-entered there as before, neither night, nor day,
going out from it, save on similar occasions.
There she neither did anything, nor acted in any
way; will and power of doing were taken away
from her. She merely enjoyed a very great
peace and happiness.

She was in this state from All Saints' Day to
the Day of St Thomas, without any new operation
taking place in her, save what follows. One
day when alone in the house, she felt herself
ravished and carried away into the air, and her
body raised from the ground. On perceiving
this, she was alarmed and cried to our Lord, and

then she found herself as to the body in the same place as before, but as to the spirit, it was carried into another region, not of this world. It seemed to her to have absolutely quitted and abandoned the body, and to have gone to its Principle and its origin, where it enjoyed a wonderful repose without however knowing or recognizing anything distinct or particular. At the end of eight days she returned to herself, but with such aloofness from all things here below, that she seemed no longer to belong to this world ; and she could not know what she had been doing during these eight days, nor who had given movement and action to her body ; in which nothing extra-ordinary had been observed, performing all its duties as usual.

But after returning to herself, she found herself as if enclosed and shut up in the heart of her divine Spouse as in her father's house, according to what he himself had made known to her. Although she there enjoyed an extreme repose, she was yet a little astonished at such a great and entire cessation of all her interior operations, which she would have liked (it seems) still to employ in acts of love as was her custom. She was maintained in this silence only from the powerlessness to do otherwise, and because her central depth was fully happy and satisfied.

H

At last our Lord willing to finish his work, and to draw her out of herself and all doubt, on the day of St Thomas, when she came to receive the Holy Communion, our Lord said to her with great authority and efficacy. " My Daughter, give up the place to me." to which she answered, " Yes, my Lord ; I wish it ; and with all my heart." At the same instant he took an entire and new possession of her, lodging himself in her heart as in his Royal Throne, and banishing and removing herself so strongly from it, that never since has she had or wished to have entry there.

She no longer regarded herself as having any right in or over herself, but as belonging entirely to her God, stripping herself of everything in him ; when anything presented itself to find entrance to her heart, she used to say to herself, " If God wishes it to enter, well and good, as for me, I have nothing to do there. He is the Master of it, and has taken its keys. Nothing of Heaven or Earth, even Angels, can have entry, if he himself does not open to them."

What is remarkable is, that at the same instant in which God said to her, " Give up the place to me," there was clearly presented to her mind all that her Director had said about the way of abandonment and self-surrender in

God, and she understood and comprehended it
all better than if she then heard it from his own
mouth ; which hitherto she had been unable to
do, namely, that in this alone was truly contained and comprehended all the perfection of a
soul, and that all which had up to this taken
place in her, very excellent and admirable as it
was, however, was as nothing in comparison
with this state, which was that his Majesty
willed her henceforth to follow. Now as his
words are efficient and never proceed without
their effect, they operated admirably in this
holy Soul ; for, from that out, she never had a
doubt on the subject, nor hesitation, but remained
firm and stedfast in this way, which brought
with it benefits beyond description.

We must make a passing remark on the excellence of this way in which God established
her ; for all the great graces he had previously
bestowed served but as preparation and disposition for this, which so far surpasses them as
the operations of God surpass those of the
creature. For these latter, however good and
excellent, are always but low and despicable in
comparison with those God effects in a Soul,
that by a willing and total abandonment of all
things strips herself freely of all herself and her
operation, to give room for that of her Beloved.

One must have the tongue and heart of the good
Armelle to worthily express this.

She could speak of it as one with experience
in both ways ; for we may say she seemed to
have reached the highest point of perfection
that a creature aided by Grace could attain
through her own operations, and yet, after having
been raised to this second state, she recognised
much contamination and much that was human
in the former, which made her say : that where-
ever the human is found, there is always defect
and imperfection, and that the greatest obstacle
Souls bring to their advancement is, that they
are not willing to allow God alone to act, but
always wish to have a share in what he does
(although in her case she could not have done
wrong in this, for as soon as God let her know
what was his will, she surrendered herself to it) ;
that her former mode of acting had been necessary to destroy and consume by the ardours
of that great fire all that was in her unsightly
to the eye of God ; but for Souls, whom from
the commencement he thus draws, there is a
great advantage, and that one cannot too early
enter on this blessed way, which makes us die
to ourselves to live only to God ; but the number
of them is small, " and the reason, I think,"
(she added) " is, a want of confidence in the

loving guidance and Providence of God ; and
secondly, the most common and ordinary, that
Souls do not wish to die to themselves or to their
own defects. It is certain that as soon as one
has given place to the divine operation, it
gradually makes known all that is displeasing
in the soul even to the smallest imperfections,
and there are few who have the courage to
combat and destroy them to the point of fidelity
which the divine light shows."

CHAPTER XVI

God having set up an absolute empire in the heart of his faithful Spouse in which he took his pleasure, and having removed and driven off all disorder, change, or agitation, rendered it formidable and terrible even to the demons, who dared not approach ; for it would have been to them an additional torment to approach the dwelling of God. And in fact, after this grace and this entrance on the new life, the first thing she experienced was that she saw herself lost and sunk down into God ; so that she was there as in a fortress utterly insurmountable.

From the day of St Thomas up to the Purification of the Holy Virgin, it seemed to her that God absorbed her daily more and more into himself and reduced her to nothingness. A little after, at the commencement of Lent, while this strong impression continued, she was reduced to such a great weakness that all vigour and strength failed her ; so that interiorly she was like one in the last agony expecting every moment the stroke of death ; and the whole of Lent she was in this state. The interior fire, according to what she told me, was so keen and penetrating that what she had previously felt was ice in comparison to this.

About three weeks before the Passion all kinds of knowledge, views, and sentiments, were taken from her mind, and the only idea remaining was the single word, Love. She could utter nothing else but this, afterwards remaining silent ; except in what was strictly required for her ordinary duty, and then it was only by great efforts. During Holy Week the assaults of divine Love so redoubled that even this single word, Love, was removed from her mind, which she then found in a state of stupidity, and she was so concentrated within, that even respiration was impeded, so that she felt as if hung up in the air while stifled or strangled. At the approach of this state, which was represented to her in an instant, nature was greatly alarmed : but the mind, being strengthened by a great ardour and vehemence, got the upperhand, and she had to undergo this cruel martyrdom, which, speaking of it, she said afterwards, was more insupportable than could be imagined.

On Good Friday these attacks redoubled and increased with such violence that they caused a species of mystic and spiritual death, and her body was reduced to such extremity from noon

to about three o'clock that one would have
thought her really deprived of life, like her divine
Saviour, who willed thus to render her participator in his sufferings and death, in order that
she might enjoy the fruits of his holy resurrection.

For on Easter Day and the following she found
herself as if raised up to a new life, feeling in
herself such a plenitude of God that, being no
longer able to contain herself, she was as if
drowned and submerged in him, feeling a new
spirit animating and governing her in every
thing, without any power in her to do otherwise
than as she was moved by him. Her body was
reduced to the state of a lifeless statue, without
movement or action but what it received from
another hand. Thus was she in regard to God,
who moved and governed her exactly as pleased
him, without resistance or opposition on her
part. From that time she allowed herself always
to be so led, being an instrument fit for and
capable of all God willed to do in her, or through
her. Her mind was deprived of action as her
body, receiving simply the various operations
God effected in her, in a manner quite passive
and divine.

She was in this state from Easter until
Ascension Sunday, without feeling anything
but that plenitude and that life of God, which

so took her out of herself and everything else
that no distinct idea, whether of God or of
creatures, occupied her, while she was wholly
lost and sunk therein, save that she felt a keen
and penetrating fire, that consumed, she said,
the centre and substance of the soul. It was
no longer with the customary violence and excess,
but with great gentleness and sweetness, which
broke up and worked nature incomparably
more than the violent impetuous assaults of the
past. She, however, said not a word, seeing
herself burned and consumed in silence after
the manner of the spirit, without plaints, groans,
or sighs, having already been in part consumed
and deadened. However, the ardour was so
strong that she almost always had fever, and
she was so upset that she hardly could speak.

The Sunday between Ascension and Pentecost,
she had a strong impression which made known
to her, that her Love and her All would not fail
to visit her on that festival. As a consequence,
she had a strong movement leading her to make
on his arrival a vow of perfect obedience to his
divine wills, and to accomplish entirely all she
should know to be to his greater glory and
honour. Meanwhile her two Directors, of whom
we have already spoken, came to Vannes on
some business. The worthy Armelle was re-

joiced at their arrival, and did not fail to tell them all that had happened with her during their absence, particularly her present disposition, and the desire of making that vow, to which she was so strongly inclined should they deem it suitable.

These Fathers were greatly pleased at learning such happy news, but yet they did not think it proper under all the circumstances that she should make the vow so soon, and they told her that if at any time hereafter the desire continued, she should inform them, and they would send her word what she should do. On this, she replied, " My Fathers, if it is not for Pentecost I think it will be on the Day of Assumption of the Holy Virgin," as it subsequently happened : but for the moment she thought no more of the matter, though she had an invincible certainty she would make it. She was so full of this sentiment that the Holy Spirit would come into her at these Festivals that she could hardly say anything to the two Fathers save the words : " In short, he will come ; yes, my Fathers, my Love and my All will come ; " and as one of them said to her, " Have you not him already ? " " Yes, I can in no way doubt it," she said, " but it matters not, I am certain he will come again, but with more abundance of graces."

From the time this impression was given until
the Monday of Pentecost she had no other
thoughts, no other words, but these : and often
without reflection, she used to utter these words
" My Lord and my All must come ; Yes ; without
doubt he will come." In a conversation of half
an hour or more with her, I think she repeated
to me more than thirty times these words,
so powerfully graven in her spirit was this
truth.

After her Directors left, the desire of making
the vow still continued, without however her
thinking on the subject or the means of executing
it, in consequence of what they had said to her.
Meantime the Festival approached, and the fire
of divine love so increased its flames that she
was ready and disposed to receive its Author
and Principle, and found herself so seized and
so bound within, that external action was
difficult for her. On the Day of Pentecost she
went early in the morning to Mass and received
Holy Communion. At the approach of this
divine fire her own kindled as usual, but not for
long ; immediately she found herself free as if
nothing had happened.

She went away to look after her household
duties, with as much ease as another could have
done, without any hindrance in her going,

coming, acting, wherever needed. This was a great effect of the goodness of God towards her, which clearly proves, what I have said elsewhere, that God seemed to watch for the times she was at leisure, to caress her and shower upon her the abundance of his holy graces. The Day of Pentecost her master entertained a great number of his relatives and others, so that the duties of the worthy Armelle were heavy, she alone having to get ready whatever was needed, and to see that everything was in good order— No small task, which required attention and freedom of mind, and this her dear Spouse gave her full and perfect.

But as soon as evening came, after she had tidied up everything, and done what was necessary in her house work, the Beloved of her heart abundantly fulfilled the promise he had given her, of coming : for in an instant he so filled her with grace and blessings, with such an infallible certainty of his divine presence, that she thought she must give up her soul, from the excess of sweetness and delight which inundated her from every side, feeling herself submerged and drowned in the indescribable and immense abyss of Love itself. She passed the whole night in these divine flames, enjoying at leisure the caresses her divine Love took pleasure in bestowing on her in the most secret centre of the heart.

The next day she went early, as usual, to the church to hear Mass and to communicate. When she was about to receive the Host, our Lord said to her lovingly, " My daughter, see how I obey thee, and do the same for me." On which, quite ardent and inflamed with love, she answered in extreme fervour, " O, yes, my Saviour and my All, I will do it with all my heart ; and for ever, if I were permitted, I would make now the vow. But, since I have not permission for it, accept my good will. You know, O my Love, the desire I have for it, but your Love itself prevents my doing it." On finishing these words she received the Holy Communion, with what sentiments of love and joy and gratitude language cannot express.

As a consequence of this grace, that plenitude of God which previously she had experienced, increased so incomparably, that there sprung up in her a great separation of her exterior action from her interior spirit ; so that she freely avowed she knew not if it was she was acting, or not ; most often the work was done, without her knowing by whom, or if she had put a hand to it ; further her soul was reduced to such a calm and tranquillity, that it seemed nothing in the

world would have been capable of troubling
her.

Moreover, since this divine fervour, her spirit
was so supple to the touch of God, that she
found herself as ready to follow his movements
as a sensual person is to follow the inclinations
of his corrupt nature. For God of his great
goodness gave her in this way the grace to accomplish perfectly that which he had engaged
her to with so much love. I say, engaged, for,
although she had not uttered the words, God
made her clearly know that he had accepted
the good will as the deed, in proof of which he
entirely took from her the desire to pronounce
her vow in word, treating it as already made.

Nevertheless, she made known all that
happened to her Father Directors, who gave
her full permission to do as she was inclined.
Therefore, on the Day of the Assumption of the
Holy Virgin, she uttered her vow of obedience,
with all the devotion and fervour and love that
a soul so forestalled with blessing as hers could
offer ; ever since, she has observed it with very
great fidelity and perfection. From that up to
All Saints' Day no new operation took place in
her, her spirit being constantly in a state of
peaceful and profound calm which kept her
concentrated within, without her being able to

act outwardly through her powers ; so utterly lost and absorbed were they. This naked and abstracted state caused some doubt as to her divine Love having left her and as if forgotten her ; for it was not usual for her to be so long without receiving assured marks of his holy presence. They were however, merely passing thoughts which had no great effect on the mind.

About the Feast of All Saints her dear Spouse, who had seemed absent since the Assumption, manifested himself to her with such abundance of love and divine joy that her heart was quite submerged in it, and in the midst of these excesses our Lord said in her inmost depth a word capable, she said, of depriving her of a thousand lives, had not his all powerful grace strengthened her to support the loving strain, " My daughter," said the divine Saviour, " You are the Daughter of Love." " Yes," she replied, " it is true, and it is through your grace and great mercy."

This favour left her so full of joy and sweetness that she was quite beside herself, and ever after to the end of her days, she was so keenly impressed thereby that she almost never lost the recollection of it ; so that she commonly spoke of herself as " The Daughter of Love," and when persons who were intimate with her wished to rejoice her, they named her, " The Daughter of

Love," to which she would reply with a feeling
of gratitude and full assurance, " Yes, doubtless
you have reason to call me the Daughter of Love,
but all is due to grace and great mercy."

After having for some days enjoyed this
sweetness and caresses, her spirit was concentrated as before in strong and simple waiting
upon God, without any distinct knowledge,
and nature on its side dragged towards the
things suitable to it, which much distressed her ;
however she took all in patience, contenting
herself with keeping a firm rein lest this same
nature should receive the slightest gratification ;
or rather, it was God who did this in her, for as
to her she was without action in anything.

On the Day of the Presentation of the Holy
Virgin this worthy Soul having freedom to think
of herself was seized by a filial and loving fear
at the sight of what had taken place, fearing
that therein might be something displeasing to
the eyes of his divine Majesty, As a remedy
she thought of making a confession, but her
Confessor saw no necessity, since there had been
no fault, and therefore she did not carry out
her design.

But having received Holy Communion, she
addressed herself with all confidence to her dear
Spouse and said to him, " O my love and my All,

it is so long since I desire to have nothing in me which opposes the purity of my love, and yet I still suffer the importunity of my nature. My Lord, you can deliver me from it, if you will; however, do not regard my request; do what shall please you." She had no sooner finished these words than she received an assurance that God had heard her, and she found it very true in the sequel; for thenceforward nature remained so subjected by this grace, that one would have judged it rather dead than mortified.

All that I have told, or at least the greatest part, took place in the year 1650, which may be called the year of grace or jubilee for her; our Lord by his mercy having made her die in a mysterious manner to all things of this world, and to all her own operations, and willed to become himself the soul of her soul and the life of her life, if I may use the expression.

Now, in order to understand what follows, you will remark that, notwithstanding all the graces and singular favours with which our Lord had been pleased to adorn and enrich the soul of his faithful Spouse, and the perfect subjection to which he had reduced all her passions, the absolute power he had given her over devils and all their artifices, at which she laughed and made less account of them than of a fly; the

I

entire death and cessation of all desires and
affections where his divine service was not concerned ; —with all that, for the space of twenty-
four years, he left a Philistine on her land
to exercise her virtue—I mean, another nature,
still drawn and inclined to seek its own little
comforts and gratifications ; and although most
often the spirit made it suffer a thousand ills,
where it thought to delight itself, it did not
yield for that, and still was trying secretly to
gain something for itself.   This was continued all
the time of which we have spoken, without her
being able to apply any remedy, which was a
great exercise of patience and much opposed
to the impetuous love that had animated her
and would have liked by a single act to burn up
and consume everything which could resist its
flames ; and which in fact had destroyed everything, save this little domestic enemy, more
troublesome than hurtful.

CHAPTER XVII

WE have remarked in the last Chapter that from the moment our Lord spake those loving words to the heart of his faithful Spouse, " My Daughter, give up the place to me," they operated very efficaciously through the free surrender she made of herself into the hands of her God, so that thenceforth all which passed between him and her up to her death I consider as holy and divine operations, where God was active, not the creature. For this reason I endeavoured to observe them with the utmost exactitude possible for me, in order that things so extraordinary might be known to all the world. And to keep more strictly to the order which God observed in communicating them, I will relate them straight on, and as they happened to her from time to time, without observing therein any method ; to show with greater clearness the proceeding of holy love in the guidance of this beautiful Soul.

From the time our Lord had delivered her from the importunity of her natural appetites, she continued very free and exempt from them ;

so that love, peace, and interior calm, increased much in her, with such a sweet and intimate union between God and her spirit that it seemed she had become " One same thing " with him. She continually felt this actual union from the Festival of the Presentation of the holy Virgin, when this grace was given, up to the Thursday before the Carnival, when her spirit found itself quite changed and overwhelmed with very great sadness and profound grief, at seeing the goodness of God so despised and offended by his creatures ; who at that season give full liberty to all kinds of vices.

This poor woman knew not what to do to stop it. She said lovingly to our Lord, " O my Love and my All, I see all men's hearts are shut against your entrance, that you are rejected and driven away by all, and that you know not in what place to make your dwelling. I offer myself to you, that you may find rest and your retreat in me." This said, it seemed to her our Lord at the same time accepted her offer ; and, in fact, he so abundantly communicated himself to her that she could not doubt of his actual presence, for he bestowed on her such tender and loving caresses that in relating it, she said it seemed God had only her alone in this world to caress, with such excessive love did he do it. To ex-

press it simply she used this comparison, that
God behaved to her like a person, who, seeking
the friendship of some others, should be rejected
by all, save one, and he being found faithful,
should alone receive all the proofs of good will
and friendship of that person. In the same way
she never failed to experience these extraordinary
caresses at the seasons, when men almost totally
forget them, to have no other God but their
sensuality.

But in the year 1651, of which we are speaking,
she received greater than usual, and love being
more kindled, the regret also, at so many offences
being committed against that adorable Majesty,
was the more keen and penetrating ; so that, to
turn aside the course of so many offences and
to prevent such evils, she offered herself to her
divine Love, affectionately supplicating him to
discharge on her all the penalties he should please
in order to prevent his being further offended.

Wonderful thing ! no sooner had she made
her offer to God than immediately by deed he
made it apparent that it was agreeable to him ;
for at the same instant she felt herself so overwhelmed with ills and pains, that there was not
a part of her body which had not its own particular torment ; so that she was compelled to
take to her bed from Friday to the following

Thursday, without any relaxation in the severity
of her sufferings, except during the time occupied
in going to a neighbouring church every morning
at six o'clock to hear Mass, and receive the holy
Communion; after which she lay down unable
to support herself. The first Thursday in Lent
her pains redoubled in such a way in the afternoon
that she thought she must die, and therefore
turning lovingly to her only Love, she said to
him : " My Lord, if you wish me to die continue
and augment my suffering; but if you wish me
still to live, give some relaxation, for I can
no longer endure." The moment she had made
this prayer, she found herself completely cured,
and as if nothing whatever had ailed her; in
proof of which she immediately got up and went
to work at her house duties.

From this we may see how prompt our Lord
was to hear the prayers of his faithful servant ;
and further, it seemed that her prayers and
sufferings turned aside the course of many sins
and debauches, for there had not passed such
a Carnival these many years back, where there
was less excess and licentiousness than in this
one. Everyone in the town was astonished, and
they said one to another, that they did not
know how it was, everybody seemed so reserved
and concentrated that there were none of the

usual recreations and diversions. I doubt not
that the sufferings of this servant of God were
the cause; to which it seems his goodness found
pleasure in granting all that she asked; and
although this I say is merely a thought of my
own, I think it nevertheless very probable, and
anyone who considers the blessings which God had
conferred on her will not find it difficult to believe.

About a week or a fortnight after she had recovered her health, she was suddenly seized with
such an ardent desire of loving Love that she was
quite dazed and lost the use of her senses, and,
seeing herself unable to satisfy her desire through
her great weakness, she became excessively sad.
Then our Lord said in the inmost depth of
her being: "I give you my Love; Love me
as much as you will." The moment she heard
these words her heart was smitten and kindled
in such a fire of Love, and it appeared so divine
and penetrating that what she had up to this
time experienced was nothing in comparison to
this, and it seemed to her, as she told me, that
she was only commencing to love as she ought
from this moment. She was some days in this
great and conscious love, which absorbed her
and filled her with divine delight and from which
nothing could distract her. When this powerful
operation had ceased her body was so weak and

broken that with difficulty could she support herself, and so the rest of Lent passed, without however her being prevented from attending to her house duties.

The Saturday before Easter our Lord made himself felt intimately present to her soul, so that all this day she was full of a great love caused by this divine presence, and having come to see me, she said, speaking of it, " It seems my Love and my All could not wait until to-morrow to rise again and make himself felt by my heart, to which he is more present than if I saw him with the eyes coming out of the Sepulchre." And speaking to her Love she said, " O my Love, you could not wait until to-morrow so eager is your goodness to do me good." The remainder of the day and night she spent in conversing lovingly with our Lord.

Next day, Easter Day, she found her heart quite changed, experiencing a certain bitterness and vexation, which would, it seemed, incline her to disquiet. This disposition much astonished her, seeing for many years back nothing similar had occurred ; particularly since the Feast of St Thomas, spoken of above. In the evening when retired to her room, she thought to herself as to the cause of this, but could settle on none, unless the permission of God to make

her know her weakness; at which she was
quite content provided his divine Majesty was
not offended, for otherwise all states were indifferent to her. While occupied with these
thoughts, an interior light clothed her in a
moment, by which she saw clearly and distinctly
what had passed in her during the day, namely
the combat between the body with all that is
earthly and sensual and the spirit with all the
celestial.

This was represented to her, as she told me,
under the appearance of two persons, one of
whom with all his strength was trying to draw
her upwards, and the other employed all his to
draw her down. This struggle went on for about
a half hour; sometimes it seemed the body,
signified by him who was drawing her down, kept
firm on the earth and was not willing to be drawn
upwards, and this she was made understand represented her inquietudes felt during the day:
at other times, the spirit had the upper hand
and drew her to itself, but gradually the body
returned towards its centre quite gently; at
last, the spirit, strengthened by Grace, drew with
such power that the body and it settled themselves in the same place and remained at peace.
Then everything disappeared and ceased.

The effects which this produced remained

with her always, for henceforth the body and
sentiments were so supple to the spirit that
they no longer hindered its operations, or to
speak more correctly, they no longer resisted
the operation of God in this holy Soul. It is
not that before this there had been other resistance than from the weakness of nature, which,
not being sufficiently strong to support the simple
and spiritual operations of the spirit, felt great
disorders through all its members when there
occurred some more extraordinary ones ; but
from that time the spirit had a complete victory
over the body and had, so to say, made it spiritual,
so that it no longer felt anything of this ; while
previously it saw itself quite softly undermined
and consumed away every day without com-
plaint or resistance.

Although we have already said that something similar had taken place when treating of
the cessation of her interior operations and of
the calm and silence God had established her in
from the commencement of that state, where we
said, she suffered divine things without resistance, there is nevertheless a great difference
between the one and the other, for in the earlier,
only the powers were deadened, and in the
second, the body and all the sentiments were so
likewise. After receiving this grace she was for

a long time apparently as if in the state of
innocence, so that had she given the rein to all
her natural appetites, they would have sought
no other thing than God, whither they inclined
of themselves, as previously they did naturally
towards the things of the world.

It would be impossible to tell the treasures
of graces and spiritual riches which this state
brought her, or the divine calm in which she
was established, being herself astonished how a
human creature could bear it : often she said to
me that if God had not supernaturally preserved
her, it would have been impossible for her to
continue in life, for this repose was so divine and
so spiritual, and approached in some sort that of
the Blessed, and was more capable of separating
soul from body than all the tortures of the world.
This great repose was caused by the subjection
of the body to the spirit and the admirable union
of her spirit itself with God : which was so great
that one day, speaking on the subject, she said
to me these words : " Though all men should
employ themselves to describe the intimate
union I feel with my divine Love, they could
never tell the least part of it.   It is so great,
yes, it is so great that the Angels themselves are
in wonder at it, and yet they do not know what
it is.   Only my God alone could tell it."

Now, as to the Angels and the Blessed, from the time she had received this last grace, our Lord made her sometimes know that she no more belonged to this world, and that Heaven was wishing for her ; and sometimes it seemed that all the Saints were inviting her to come to share the celestial dwelling, and she used to say to them, " In vain you show me your delights : I have no desire to enjoy them but when my Love wills, my Paradise is to accomplish his adorable will."

Meantime, though she was in such a perfect conformity that she would not have wished by a moment to advance or retard the hour of her decease, she no longer regarded herself as a person of this world, and often said, " I have nothing to do here below, nothing detains me but the will of my God, for on my part, I have done what he had ordained me. I am quite ready to depart when it shall please him ; for he sent me into this world only that I might love him, and through his great mercy I have so strongly loved him, that it is not possible for me to love him more in the manner of mortals. I must go to him to do it in the way of the Blessed. Other times she would say : " Between God and me there is only the fragility of this poor body, which is so undermined and consumed from loving that it needs but a little puff of air to snap and break it up utterly."

Such was her usual language from the time God had reduced her to the state we have just described, in which she long remained, and when it pleased his Majesty to confer on her some new grace or favour, she did not for that pass from one state to a different one, but continued steady and fixed in this : and then she enjoyed more distinctly and more really the greatness of the Beloved, through very profound concentrations and very delicate touches, which he effected in the very centre of her soul, and which, owing to their being so spiritual and divine, admitted of no description. She used only to say, that a single one of those touches far surpassed all she had had up to that time.

Notwithstanding she had reached such a high degree of perfection, the Devil did not consider himself totally conquered, and at this time made a new effort to see if he could in any way trouble the peace and repose of this Soul. He therefore tried to frighten her with vain fears to withdraw her from the great calm she enjoyed, but his attempts were useless, and served only to make known to the heart of this happy woman that God had given her full power over the desires and sensualities of nature, when he had by special grace freed her from its importunity and had moreover perfectly subjected the body to the spirit, rendering it in its way as if a participator in the qualities of this same spirit. Besides this, he wished further to make her victorious over this last enemy, who for many years had not dared to appear; which was done in the way you will now see.

One day about the Feast of the Assumption of the holy Virgin, when retired to take rest, she had a strong idea of the tender and loving caresses she used formerly to offer her Beloved, at the time it was in her power to exhibit the excess of her love, and the favours she in return used to receive from him, and the way in which she had cleared and overcome so many ambushes of her enemies, in his name and by his strength. While so thinking a gentle doze fell on her, and she saw herself shut up in a chamber while she held in her arms a little infant, that she embraced and cherished with great tenderness. In the midst of her caresses two men presented themselves with exceedingly dirty garments and horrible gestures, who wanted to outrage her, and used all their efforts to make her leave the child and look them in the face. But they could do neither the one nor the other, at which they exhibited extreme rage, particularly because she would not condescend to lift her eyes to look at them.

After some time had thus passed, getting weary, she rose and went out of the chamber to avoid their importunities. When she went out she knew not what became of the child, but it seemed to her she had received from it such power of spirit, that she would have conquered Hell, had it presented itself. Continuing her road, she found herself in a great plain, where these two men still pursued her, playing a thousand monkey tricks round her. They even gave her blows to disquiet her if they could; but she paid no more attention to them than if they had done nothing. At last one of them, vexed at his useless attempts, said to the other : " Let us leave her ; do we not see all our efforts are thrown away, we shall gain nothing ; it is better for us to take ourselves off." But the other, more obstinate than ever, continued still, without however having power to touch her. He tried only to make her turn back to look at him.

Seeing that he persisted, and finding herself strengthened with an extraordinary vigour, she turned towards him and, seizing him by the neck threw him on the ground, without however any emotion ; and animated by a courage quite divine, she trampled him under foot, and after

beating him soundly she threw him into some
stagnant water near by. When he tried to get
out of this she gave him several blows with a
knife she found at hand, until he no longer
appeared, and everything vanished. She immediately awoke, her heart so full of love and
divine glory that it seemed to her she was already
in Paradise.

Whoever will examine the thing closely will
notice that all which she saw in the dream was a
simple representation of what had taken place
during the course of her life ; (as she many times
admitted to me) for that tender love she had for
the child was none other than the ardent love
she always had for our Lord Jesus Christ, whose
sacred Humanity she had so constantly before her
at the commencement, that she almost never lost
it from sight. This doubtless gave her strength
easily to surmount all the snares of Satan. And
when advancing on the road of perfection, she
lost this sensible presence of the holy Humanity
of the Son of God, he communicated to her
another of his Divinity, far more spiritual and
intimate, so that the Devil could approach it only
at a distance, all the avenues of her heart being
completely closed. As to her not looking at the
face of those men, it is the genuine and faithful
practice she observed all her life in regard to the

suggestions and temptations of the enemy, which
she never considered to examine them, but
despised all; without even consenting to hear
them, her spirit being so occupied with loving
that it could dwell on nothing else.

CHAPTER XVIII

AFTER this holy woman had won the signal
victories described, God established her in the
power and possession of his wealth, that is to
say, he made known to her the great treasures
of graces and divine riches she had acquired
by having sustained and surmounted so many
attacks for his love. She saw herself so abound-
ing in goods and delights that she reposed therein,
like one who, having toiled and sweated many
years and undergone great labours, has at length
acquired such riches that he sees himself no
longer in need of anything, and has become so
powerful that he no longer dreads the approach
of any enemy.

So it was with her, and she used these terms
to explain her state. "All my wealth is," she
said, "God alone; and now that by his great
mercy and goodness he is entirely mine, as I am
entirely his, I have no need to labour to acquire
new things. I have merely to repose in his
goods; and as he reposes in me, so I repose in
him, being entirely shut up and annihilated in
him. There I no more find myself, and when I
146

say that *I enjoy*, that *I love*, and that *I possess*,
it is not *I* who receive that ; it is his love which
is my love ; his riches are my riches ; his peace
is my repose ; his ways are my delights ; and
so with the rest of his divine perfections. And
now there remains nothing for me to desire ;
for I am quite loaded with goods I have no fear
of losing, for they belong purely to my Love and
my All ; and on my part I no longer possess them
as from my selfhood, so there is no fear of their
being taken away." Such were her admirable
discourses at this time, or rather those which
the force and strength of her Love made her
utter ; for otherwise she would have said nothing
of them, but our Lord, who willed that these
treasures of grace should be manifested, permitted her so to announce them in order that
they should be recorded.

At this same time she happened one
day, thoughtlessly, to say something amusing to
divert those with whom she was ; at the same
moment she was interiorly checked for it, and
her Love made her know that henceforth her
tongue was a blessed tongue, consecrated to his
divine Majesty, and that she should have no
other employment for it than that which the
Blessed in Heaven have, praising him incessantly ;
that her life should be pure as that of the Angels,

and her love great and burning as that of the
Seraphim. And as to will and to do is the
same thing with God, at the same instant she
experienced the effects of his divine volitions ;
particularly in the matter of Love, of which a
flame so great and divine shed itself through
her heart that she said : " From that time forward
nothing is felt in this heart but a living and
celestial flame, which never abates and which
consumes without destroying me, after the
manner of the Seraphim in Paradise, who are
consumed by the sweet violence of their love."

Some days after she went to confession for
having said that idle word, which was the
greatest fault she had committed for a long time ;
so pure was her heart. Her Confessor after
confession said to her the same words as our
Lord had said on the subject, and that her tongue
should no longer be employed save in blessing
and glorifying God, like the Blessed. She was
greatly rejoiced and said to him, " My Father,
you only confirm the truth of the lights which
God has given me in this matter." Then she
related to him all that had taken place ; finding
therein a new cause of praise and love for her
God in his great care and goodness towards her.

He gave her a further very signal proof of it
on the Octave of the Nativity of the holy Virgin

in this same year 1651. One morning, while at
church hearing Mass, her mind was suddenly
carried away in a consideration of all the nations
of the earth. She saw them, some deprived of a
knowledge of the true God, which caused her
extreme regret ; others, where many persons of
holy life were at the price of their blood en-
deavouring to carry the light of Faith among
these poor blind ones, and this gave her great
joy ; others again in Christendom, some of
whom live in obedience to the commandments
of God, while some despise them and pay no
attention.

All these particulars, I say, presented themselves to her mind and produced in her heart
suitable effects—some of joy, others of sadness ;
and she felt for all equally a very great love,
which led her to recommend all alike to his
divine Love, that his goodness would be pleased
to confirm in good those already in it, and withdraw from evil those who were plunged therein.
While she was in the intensity of her prayer, she
suddenly lost all knowledge and views she had
had on the subject, exactly as if a curtain had
been drawn before her eyes to hinder her seeing.
At the same time our Lord made himself perceived, present in the inmost depth of her soul,
and in his usual way said to her, as though jealous

of the love of his Beloved, " My Daughter, love
me alone." Then she answered with very great
ardour, " Yes, my Love, I wish it ; Yes, I wish
it, I wish it "; and during the whole of the Mass
she could not hinder herself uttering interiorly
these words, " I wish it, I wish it," with a love
and fire indescribable.

She went to receive the holy Communion still
uttering these words, which were then changed
into these terms, " At last Love is enclosed and
shut up ; at last Love is shut in and enclosed."
And these words stuck to her heart, which
she kept uttering continually, like the preceding
ones, until the close of the Mass ; then, as she
was returning home, midway on her road, they
ceased, and at the same instant our Lord produced an operation so sweet and loving in the
inmost of her soul, that it was a wonder she did
not drop to the ground. He made her then
see that just as all himself, who is Love essential
and infinite, was shut in and enclosed in her, so
he willed to make her pass, to transform and
incorporate her, into himself, and at the moment
she found herself as if dead and deceased in the
immense love of the Divinity.

To tell what she now experienced is impossible.
She herself knew not what to say of it, unless
that one could absolutely tell nothing of it. She

returned to the house, where all she could do
was to throw herself on a bed, and she was for
the space of three days under this wonderful
operation, after which she was able to go about
where necessary for external matters; but as
to the spirit, it was always in the same place.
And, as her life was God himself, so did she
participate in her manner in the qualities of the
Divinity; for since she received this favour
things, which formerly had caused her joy or
sadness, no longer produced their effects in the
usual way; for example, before she received
this grace when God was offended, it was to her
insupportable, and she was so displeased that
she often fell ill: on the other hand when she
saw him loved and obeyed, she received inconceivable joy.

But after receiving this grace, she no longer
felt things in this way; natural sentiments and
the passions were entirely extinguished. She
saw evil and had it in horror, feeling a total
estrangement from it; but it was without sadness and without pain; so all which turned to
the glory of her Beloved gave her joy, but
without emotion or any demonstration—it was
a joy perfect and divine, which could not receive
diminution or alteration from anything here
below—a joy, in short, which had its source in

the true and essential joy—that is God himself;
as regards the other passions, it was exactly the
same as with these two.

The following All Saints' Day her divine Love
willed to give her some knowledge of the glory
and felicity which those glorious Souls enjoy in
Heaven, and by a supernatural light he made
her see how these Blessed Spirits never separate
from Love nor the presence of their Beatific
Object. As she was admiring their happiness in
this, her spirit was at the same moment led to
deplore the misery of those who live here below,
in the continual danger and hazard of falling
from Grace, however high a state of it they may
possess. While these views seemed to lead her
to a kind of compassion and apprehension for
the loss of so many Souls, who cast themselves
into sin, far from taking the trouble to withdraw
themselves from it, our Lord made her know,
how on his part he was quite ready to aid them
to escape from such misfortune; and she seemed
to see him with infinite love offering his divine
hands to all, to those in a good state, in order to
maintain them therein, and to those who were
not, to establish them therein; and she saw
that it was only those who gave their hands to
those of this divine Saviour and who kept firmly
attached to them, who could avoid the rocks

and dangers that follow us and surround us from
all sides in this mortal life.

At this a very tender desire sprang up in her
soul never to quit that divine hand and to follow
his guidance in all things. Her divine Love
gave her the assurance of this, and made her
know, that for her there was nothing to dread,
as his mercy would never abandon her; and in
proof of what he said, he presented his blessed
hand, which she clasped and tightly grasped,
joining one of hers to it. For three or four days
it seemed to her that in reality she was constrained to carry her hand to her mouth, in
order to kiss and adore the hand of Jesus, which
was joined with hers. This was not the only
favour she received.

Her dear Love, who had made her see a sample
of the glory of the Blessed, willed also to make
her a participator in her manner; so that, as
what she had most admired in the felicity of the
Saints, was that great love and that continued
vision which they have of the Divinity, and
which constitutes the essence of their beatitude;
so our Lord also conferred on her this grace, by
making her contemplate in herself his glory and
his divine attributes, and above all, his infinite
Love, with such clearness that she became quite
deified and transformed into him. It seemed

to her that she had become " one same thing
with him."

This made her use the following admirable
and profound language, " Now, God is all, and as
for me, I am no longer : I am through his mercy
returned whence I had come forth. He alone
lives and reigns in me, and no longer I ; for I
am no longer in me, but in him ; where I no
longer find myself and where I am lost. It is he
alone who is alive, for I no longer see anything
which is not himself." Here are word for word
her very phrases that I many times heard from
her own mouth ; from which we may judge to
what a state this happy creature had attained.

On St Andrews' Day God, continuing still to
bestow on her new favours, made her feel a love
so pure, so sweet, and so divine, that it seemed
to her she had never yet experienced the like ;
so that she said to God, " I know not my Love
and my All, why you confer on me such graces,
for it appears you find every day new ways
of caressing me and showing me you love me.
If anyone knew what your Goodness makes me
feel, he would say that you have only me to look
after, and that you are idolizing your poor and
mean creature." Certainly she had good reason
to speak so, for in truth God bestowed on her
inconceivable favours and caresses.

It seemed to her at this time that she continuously heard the voice of the Beloved saying,
"Thou art no longer in the winter : the winter
is passed for thee and will never return"; and
this voice made itself heard in the inmost depth
of her heart from St Andrews' Day until the eve
of the Conception of the holy Virgin, when she
found herself overwhelmed with great pains in
all her limbs, which however had no influence
on her spirit. A day or two previously she had
had a conversation with the Rector of the College
of Jesuits, with whom, since the departure of her
Director, she had been in communication, and
as she related to him what had taken place since
her last interview, she told him among other
things that she often heard these words, "There
is no more winter for her, that it was already
passed." On this the Father replied with a
smile : "Do not imagine that, my Daughter :
no, the winter is not yet passed. You are at
present in the spring, and the time of flowers ;
but the winter will return again, and you will
yet feel it."

She heard these words without paying any
more attention to them than to an ordinary
remark in conversation, and until the Day of
the holy Virgin she retained no notion of them.
On that day at three or four o'clock in the

morning she was awakened, and, smitten with a
great love, she heard distinctly spoken in the
inmost of her soul by our Lord. " No, my
Daughter : thou art not in the time of flowers :
for flowers are too inconstant : it needs but a
frost or a hail shower to beat them down, or too
much heat or wind to wither them. Thou art
not like that ; thou art a ripe fruit. And as
the ripe fruit is gathered and stored in a secret
place, all thou hast done in thy life is stored in
Heaven. But when the fruit has been gathered
we must take care from time to time that it
does not spoil ; for if once it decay, it is cast
away as worthless ; so do thou be careful to
remain always faithful and submissive to my
wills. Do not, however, fear that thou canst
ever incur the misfortune of falling, for I will
preserve thee always through my mercy as a
fruit I have gathered and reserved for myself
alone."

These are the words our Lord said to her,
which are as loving as full of instruction.
Accordingly she drew from them admirable
lessons as to the fidelity we owe to Grace ; and
how in this world to whatever height of perfection his Grace may have elevated us, it is
only on God's goodness and mercy we should
ever rely. As to the vivid impressions of love

she received, they are incredible, and they influenced even her body, so that she was immediately delivered from the pains she was
before suffering, and so concentrated and shut
up interiorly that nothing of the exterior could
be felt. Thus she continued until the Saturday
before the last week in Advent. On that day,
her diverse occupations required attention of
mind, and therefore that powerful concentration
in which love had kept her ceased, so that
she was able to attend to everything necessary,
without any hindrance.

In this freedom she remained until the
following Tuesday, when her extraordinary business ceased. In the early morning she went
to hear Mass, and when about to receive the
holy Communion, our Lord showed her that she
was like those prisoners who are allowed to
go out occasionally to look after their business,
which finished, they have to return to their
former dwelling place : in exactly the same way
he wished again to confine and shut her up in the
prison of his Divinity. On the same instant
she found herself enclosed and shut into God in
a way that baffled all description. The love
and ineffable sweetness, which this divine favour
caused her, drew from the depth of her heart
these loving words addressed to our Lord, " O

my Love, and my All ! You are then the
Jailor of my heart who hold it captive and
prisoner !" Then she remained silent, enjoying
at leisure the wonderful delights of her charming Prison.

The next day some trifling occurrence diverted
her a little from this profound peace in which
she was plunged, although the thing was so
trifling that she hardly perceived it. This
happened only to open a door for the favour
which God willed to bestow on her ; for, as soon
as this slight movement came to attack her
heart ; her divine Love who reposed there, or
rather who had shut her up in himself, said these
words, " My Daughter, when a person is retired
into his house with his intimate friend, with
whom he is in familiar conversation, if any
intruder comes to knock at the door, he makes
no semblance of hearing him, or else sends word
that he is engaged and therefore in private ; so
oughtest thou to do with everything which may
offer itself ; for thou art no longer for anything
in this world but for me alone." To this she
replied, " O my Love, yesterday I called you my
Jailer, but to-day I will name you my Door-
keeper, the Guardian of my heart and the Light
of my soul ; for doubtless it is you who perform
all these offices on my behalf, and you enlighten

and instruct me through ways and means I should never have thought of."

It was with very good reason she spoke thus; every day God gave her new knowledge, which so kindled the fire of divine Love in her soul that at this period she used ordinarily to say: " If there was the smallest part of me which subsisted through Self, long ago the vehemence of this Love would have destroyed it, but as I do not see it at all in me and it is all in God, from whom it goes not out to communicate itself to me (so am I lost and submerged in him); I subsist therefore and carry on my life through the strength he gives me, until it may please him to cut short its course, which will be when it shall please him: for as for me, there is no longer, through his great mercy, anything which arrests me in this world."

The following Thursday, which was St Thomas's Day, our Lord bestowed a singular favour, surpassing the last two, inasmuch as the comparison he used expressed more fully the inseparable union between him and her. On this day, after receiving the Communion, he told her that he wished her to be like those little snails, who wherever they go carry their house and dwelling with them and never leave it: when anything strikes or attacks them they conceal themselves, and so retire within that one sees only their shell, they themselves no longer appearing ; thus he wished himself to be her dwelling-house, her place of refuge, whence she would no more go out, that in all places and all circumstances he would conceal her and shut her up within himself, in order that nothing should any longer appear in her, save himself alone.

At the same time she found herself more than ever shut up in that divine dwelling, with a knowledge so clear and so certain of the greatness, excellence, and beauty of the place where she was, that she cried out with all her heart: " O my dear Love, it is two years since by your great mercy you gave me entrance into your house, whence you have never permitted me to go out for a single moment, and yet it seems to me I have only just entered, so much I see and know that I had never yet known or perceived." This she said because of the admirable views of his divine perfection God opened out to her, which hitherto she had not discovered.

God had behaved in her case like a kind father, who keeps his son in his house and shows him a thousand marks of tenderness and friendship in all circumstances ; but who yet does not display before him his treasures and riches until he has

attained an age, when he is able to value them
at their true price.   Thus this holy Soul, although
for such a long time she had her dwelling in the
heart of God, if we may so speak, and was lodged
there as in her own house, yet Love kept her so
powerfully occupied that she could do nothing
else but love ; but after God had bestowed on
her this last grace, there hardly passed a day
when he did not give her new light, to make
her understand the marvels of the place of her
dwelling.   This did not turn her aside from her
love, but inflamed her still more and more ; so
that she was overcome by it, and all this week
she was almost obliged to keep her bed after
receiving the holy Communion ; or at least, to
retire into some corner, where she remained so
feeble that she could scarcely move, though
feeling no pain, and she seemed to herself
to have neither body nor soul, but only an
incredible Love which converted her wholly into
itself.

On Christmas Day while hearing Mass there
arose in her an intense and penetrating desire,
that her Beloved should take birth in the hearts
of all men ; and for this result she conjured him
to do so with such profound affection, that it
seemed to her that the Holy Spirit was the Author
of her prayer, and that he furnished reasons and

L

motives to bend the divine clemency to show
them that mercy; although she knew that God,
on his side, was quite ready to do it, but that on
their part, very few were disposed to receive it,
inasmuch as by their sins and attachment to
things of this world, they shut the door of their
hearts and refused him entrance.

While these things were occupying her spirit
she went to receive the Host, without almost
perceiving it and without feeling her ordinary
delights; she merely continued still the same
prayer, and when she was outside the church on
her return home, it occurred to her that she had
communicated as I have just told; and being
astonished how it could have been, she said to
our Lord, " O my divine Love, to-day you came
into me secretly and surreptitiously without
making yourself known; but it is vain for you
to hide, I know well that I have received you."
She did not say this by way of regret at his having
so used her, for she was so indifferent that she
did not give a thought whether God caressed
her or not, being so possessed of him that she
never reflected on what he was doing in her,
unless he himself caused her to do so. This he
did only to give an entrance to new graces,
as appeared in the present instance, for no
sooner was she arrived at home than God

made himself felt to her soul with such sweetness that she thought her last day had come, for it seemed her whole nature was about to dissolve away. All the remaining days of the year thus passed.

CHAPTER XIX

On New Year's Day at dawn her heart was seized on her awakening with a bright flame of love which seemed to set her all on fire, together with a certain presentiment that doubtless her Beloved willed to give her a New Year's gift on that day, without, however, knowing in what fashion or manner it would be ; for her heart was so full that it did not seem to her to be capable of receiving more. None the less she had a strong conviction that he reserved for her some further signal favour : sometimes without thinking she kept saying, " My Love, I believe you wish this morning to give me my New Year's gift."

When at Mass she was given a full knowledge of the grandeur and perfections contained in the most holy Name, JESUS, and of the ardent desire which God has to save and deliver all men from the miserable servitude of sin. To contribute to it on her part, she endeavoured with all her power through a very fervent Love to incite the divine Goodness to give to all the faithful, but especially those present at the Mass, the grace of

participating in the fruits and merits of this most
holy Name, and that it might have full effect in
them.

The nearer the time for holy Communion the
more the mysteries of his August Name were
opened up and disclosed to her, and the love of
this Name kindled so powerfully in her soul that
she had much difficulty in containing herself.
But after communicating it was quite other
flames, for our Lord made himself intimately
perceived by her, making her see with the eyes
of the soul, more clearly than she could have
done with the eyes of the body, that he was
graving with his divine hand and imprinting
in the depth of her heart his most adorable
Name, Jesus, which remained with her ever
since imprinted in a manner so admirable and
so incomprehensible, that she afterwards declared, none but he who engraved it could tell
the excellence of this grace ; which loaded her
with such love that all this day and the following
ones she spoke only of the grandeur of this divine
Name : for to everyone she could speak to she
said in a tone quite seraphic, " Give, give your
hearts to Jesus, that he may there imprint his
holy Name, He asks only that, and is quite ready
to do it for all who will give themselves up to
him. Yes, give them to him, that he may make

of them whatever he pleases." She uttered
these words with such zeal that all in the house
were astonished ; for she was not used to show
outwardly what was passing within. They said
to one another, that doubtless Armelle had received some special grace that day, and that it
seemed Jesus was in her heart and on her lips.

Not without ground they spoke thus, for it
was indeed imprinted there and made her utter
these loving words which she addressed to him :
" O my Love and my All, undoubtedly you have
given me my New Year's gift, and you could not
help caressing me on the first day of this year.
It seems that you have your delight only when
you do good to me, and that you could not pass
a single day without conferring on me new
graces." For about a fortnight she was in these
raptures of love which that favour had caused.
At the end of that time our Lord, who wished
to do good to a certain Soul, gave Armelle so
great a desire for her salvation, that day and
night she had no other thought but of com-
mending that person to him ; so that sometimes
she said, " I believe my Love, that you wish me
to forget you and myself to have no other care
but of this Soul ; it seems my life and my health
depend only on that." What made her speak thus
was, that since God had given her this strong

impulse, her physical strength was so feeble that with difficulty could she support herself.

She came to see me at this time, and speaking of her health she said she was much better than usual, because she saw people trying to reconcile themselves to our Lord, and that this brought her as much relief as would an excellent remedy to a person extremely ill; that yet her perfect cure would never come in this world, for her divine love was always much offended here. "Many times I said to him," continued she, "within the last fortnight, that if he wished me to be no longer ill, he should bring all the world to love him, acknowledge him and serve him, and that then I should be in good health, and as happy as one who saw his intimate friend triumph over all his subjects." "It seems," she further said to me, "that my divine Love no longer leaves me in the world but to procure his honour, and that I have no other business but seeing if his glory is increased; this is my whole employment, and I do not work at it like a servant for his master, but as a spouse in the property of her husband, which she regards as their common property, nothing between them being separate. And to tell you truth I do not see myself at all in this, but God alone, in whom I am so plunged that most times I believe I have

neither life nor mind, but that they are lost in
him, who alone supplies all this to me, and thus
his honour, his glory, his insults, are mine : all
that concerns him in short is all mine, as I
am all his." Thus she often spoke to me,
and indeed it was almost impossible for her to
speak of anything else, for it was her genuine
life, and what she experienced every day with
such clearness, that it seemed God wished to
make her one of the Blessed even in this world.

On the third Sunday in Lent, having risen
very early and finding all those in the house
still reposing, she said to herself that she also
would have hers with her dear Love, and placing
herself on her knees beside her bed, she adored
the most holy Trinity by reciting three *Paters*
and three *Aves*, as was her wont every morning.
She had hardly finished them when the most
holy Trinity manifested itself to her in an incomprehensible manner. As to that which these
three adorable Persons made further known to
her of their divine perfections ; it was Love.
There the Eternal Father made her see that the
infinite Love he bore to men had obliged him to
give his Son for their redemption ; the Son
made known to her that the Love he bore them
had urged and forced him to become man and
to suffer all the torments of his Life and Passion ;

the Holy Spirit made her understand that he, who is infinite Love, had given himself to them through this same love, and that he would give himself to them until the end of the world, in order to draw out all their Love. Afterwards they made her see that all Three were only One in Essence, and that they gave themselves to men to make them all similar. This grace and favour she received on that day; on which I can say only what she said, that, if the powerful hand of God did not greatly strengthen a Soul, it would be impossible for her to live after such revelations. Therefore she said to our Lord: " O my dear Love, what a great furnace you have kindled to burn me! I do not know but that I shall still feel it a week hence!" This she said with reference to that grace, and because when she thus received special ones, she used to be for some time in such a state, that the thing would be as present to her, and the love as inflamed, as when it had taken place.

CHAPTER XX

On Palm Sunday, at waking, her heart was seized with violent grief accompanied by a great love, reflecting that the triumph and magnificent reception on this day accorded to her Saviour had been but to enhance the insult and disgrace of the death he suffered a few days later, and desiring to bear in her body as well as in her spirit the pains of her only Love, she asked to share in them. This she instantly obtained ; for she felt very great pains in all her body and in the heart a flame so quick and penetrating that she was compelled to keep her bed that and the two following days. One Tuesday this flame in her heart spread over her whole body, so that it seemed to her that her bed and every thing she touched was a burning fire which consumed her to the marrow of her bones, and at the same time God made her know that he willed her body as well as her spirit to be the sacrifice and victim of love to be burned with its flames. Then she cried to him with all her strength, " O my Love and my All! You know that through your great mercy I will all that you

will, and that there is nothing in me which is
not yours, and that if I knew that the smallest
part of my flesh or the smallest bone of my body
was opposed to your holy wills, I would instantly cut or tear it off and cast it away to
the crows, or on a dung hill." She had hardly
finished when this great fire withdrew and collected in her heart as before and left her body
relieved and refreshed. "It seemed," she told
me, "that God only asked of me this submission to his divine wills to afford me relief ; and
although he knew well through his grace I would
not contradict him, he yet wished thereby to
oblige me to assure him of it, and further to make
me recognize the obligations I was under to his
goodness, seeing that everything was submissive
and subjected in me."

On the Wednesday and Thursday of this same
week she was a little stronger than the previous
days, the cause of which was, that she had found
the means of assisting some utterly destitute
sick poor who were perishing of poverty and
want ; for having obtained her mistress's leave
she went to visit them, supplied them with good
food, and with the help of pious and charitable
persons procured for them the aids of the Holy
Sacraments.

This circumstance, I say, had quite strength-

ened and invigorated her, as she confessed
to me; but it was not for long, for from
Thursday night to Good Friday the flames of
divine love redoubled more than before, and
all the torments of her Saviour were so vividly
represented to her that there was not one in
which she did not assist in spirit as if she were
present at the place and time he endured them.
The pain she conceived was so great that three
times on this morning, she afterwards declared,
she saw herself on the point of expiring. I
questioned her if she did not then desire the
assistance of anyone, or to receive the Sacraments; but she told me, that finding herself
in the arms of Love, entirely sunk and absorbed
in him, she had no other movement than to let
him do whatever he should please, being as well
inclined to death as to life.

About midday her divine Love withdrew her
spirit from the view of his torments on earth
to make her see them in Heaven as the Blessed
contemplate them. She seemed to see all the
Court of Heaven filled with joy and cheerfulness
at the great Victory, which God had won over
his enemies on this holy day, and that, in the
sacred and divine person of his Son, they had all
triumphed. She also saw Jesus Christ, who, all
covered with blood and wounds, showed himself

to them in that state, and was clothed with his
wounds as with a vesture of glory and honour,
which gave a marvellous brilliance to his divine
countenance, and an inexpressible happiness to
all the Blessed. At the same time her loving
Saviour invited her also to contemplate him in
this way and to share in the common joy of all
Heaven. Thus she passed the rest of the day,
smitten with a very powerful and penetrating
fire of love.

After all this, her body became wearied and
ill, and as she needed a little rest to gain strength,
God made manifest in this, as in all other circumstances, the care he had of her and what
affected her ; for during some days he abated
the ardour of her flames, which were consuming
her and destroying her body, and he left her
from Holy Saturday to Easter in a state quite
suited to her indisposition, without her spirit
experiencing anything that could in the least
affect her. I was astonished to see her so
indifferent and the heart void of that extraordinary love, which ordinarily she used to experience at these holy solemnities. She told me
I should not be surprised, that the cause was
simply that she needed it that her body might
gain a little strength, and that it was not the
first time her divine Love had a care not only of

her soul but of her body also, that he willed to be
its Physician, and that she had observed, since
to please him she had given up her wages and
everything she had, and no longer had the means
of paying for a physician or medicine, that he
had undertaken this charge.

Then breaking out in wonder at the goodness
of Love towards her, she cried, " See what excess
of goodness ! A God deigns thus to have the
care of his mean creature ! How after this not
die and consume away from Love ? For the
more frail and despicable I am in myself, the
more God takes care of me, even in the smallest
things. It is enough to ravish my spirit in
admiration. Oh ! how good it is to abandon
oneself, to cast oneself into the arms of Love !
Who can tell the care he has of those who do
it with all their heart ? Oh ! undoubtedly only
he and they ; for the world is incapable of con-
ceiving such great excess of love and goodness."

Some days afterwards, having gone to see her
Director and speak to him, her heart and mind
were so seized upon and plunged in love that she
thought she would be unable to say a word, and
reflecting as to what she could say to her Director
when he came, for she was in the College Church
waiting for him, and being a little troubled on
the point, our Lord who watched all her thoughts,

gave her a light thereon, and made her very clearly hear in the substance of her soul these two words, "My Daughter, I am thy Speech and thy Silence." Having heard these words spoken quite to the point, and marvelling at the excessive goodness of God towards her she was smitten with such a wonderful love that she almost fell in a faint, so that she was constrained to support herself against the wall. Her Director came when this great excess was a little over, and she told him the words our Lord had made her hear, which served as the opening for a discourse quite celestial and divine.

It is true that these words were so loving and full of mysteries that they were capable of bursting the heart, for she said, " Who is there could, unless supported by God, bear without dying such favours ? That a God should say to his paltry creature, " *I am thy Speech and thy Silence.*"

What these words effected in her soul besides this great love was, that ever after she took no trouble about her words or her silence ; since God through the excess of his goodness was willing to be for her both the one and the other, and thenceforward she began to feel their effects ; for her soul was afterwards in a continual silence up to Corpus Christi, without any interruption

of any kind either on the part of God or her own ;
only from time to time the great love which
burned in the depth of her soul cast out flames
more quick and penetrating than usual ; but
this took effect in silence on the part of both,
and thus she continued up to Tuesday after
Trinity Sunday. On that day, being with a
person to whom she used to speak freely of the
most secret things of her soul, this person de-
signedly put her on the great mercies with which
God had anticipated her.

After a sufficiently long conversation on this
matter the worthy woman went home, her mind
quite filled with the blessings God had so
abundantly bestowed on her, in addition to which
was the holy Eucharist, the festival of which
was soon to be celebrated ;—these considerations kindled such a fire in her soul that she said
it could set fire to hearts of ice or of marble.
" And as it is impossible," continued she, " that
a Soul which truly loves, seeing herself anticipated with such graces, and that a God wills to
do so much for her, should not have also on her
side an extreme desire to do something for him,
and to employ herself and quite consume herself
in love, I found myself in this disposition at that
time ; addressing myself to my God, I said to
him from the depth of my soul, ' O my divine

Love! is there not anything still for me to do
or to destroy to please you? and could I not
show in some fashion the love I bear you? Is
there anything still for me to do? Tell it to
me and I will accomplish it though I should lose
a thousand lives.' As I was saying these words,
the following were said to me with such efficacy
that I doubt not it was our Lord said them,
'Nothing at all,' and he repeated, 'Nothing,
nothing at all, except to abandon yourself and
to let me act.' At these words everything grew
peaceful and calm in my soul, and I could do
nothing but remain overwhelmed under the yoke
and gentle burden of Love and die from its
flames." These are the very words in which
she related to me this favour which our Lord
had shown her.

Before proceeding further it is necessary for
the intelligence of what follows to explain the
general and ordinary disposition of mind in
which God had for a long time kept her; but
which was extraordinarily increased from the
opening of the Jubilee on the twenty-fifth of
February in the year Sixteen hundred and fifty-
two. This disposition was a continual view of
the offences and insults which are committed
every moment against the Sovereign Majesty of
God, which caused such sensible and piercing

M

grief in her soul, that she often said death would
be a thousand times easier to endure than to
see her divine Love thus outraged by sinners :
on the other hand, she felt such compassion that
incessantly she claimed for them the divine
Mercy, praying that it might enlighten the eyes
of their soul, that they might recognize the
precipice and misery awaiting them. God gave
her wonderful knowledge on this matter, which
made her utter words quite flaming, as well on
the infinite goodness of God in bearing with
sinners, as on the infinite malice of sin, and the
blindness and stupidity of those that allow
themselves to be carried away by it, and have
no other pleasure but in offending infinite Love,
who makes them incessantly feel the effects of
his liberality and mercy.

Her mind amidst all these lights was placed
in this state, which lasted from the commencement of the Jubilee until God introduced her
into another state, that we shall mention below ;
to which the former served as a preparation.

It seemed to her, that God had appointed her
between him and them that she should obtain
their peace and reconciliation with his divine
Majesty ; for which she was employed in a
manner so high and elevated, with a compassion
so piercing and so loving for these poor sinners,

that it seemed she was feeling in truth something of the pains and anguish which the Son of
God felt at the sight of sins while he was in the
world, and after his example she strove to obtain
their pardon and to pacify divine justice, using
for the purpose supplications so touching and
living, that it was clear she had no other
principle but the Holy Spirit, who constrained
her to this. Usually she used to say " My dear
Love and my All, pardon them for they know
not what they do," and much else which was
spoken not by words, but which an interior voice
and affection incessantly kept uttering in the
deepest centre of her soul.

Her soul was established as an intermediary
between God and sinners, feeling vividly the
interests of both; but those of God were far
stronger than those of men, and therefore she
would have wished with all her heart to destroy
sin and to prevent its ever being committed in
the world. One day in the height of her love,
she made prayers and entreaties to the Eternal
Father, that by the merits of his Son he would
destroy and annihilate sin, drawing all Souls to
his Love and the knowledge of him by any manner
whatsoever, provided he was no longer offended.
In the very height of her entreaty, she heard
the voice of God speak to her these words,

" That it was a decree, given in the tribunal of his divine Wisdom, that men should continue in their free, unfettered, choice, to love him or to offend him ; and that according to that decree he could not force them, nor violate their freedom : but that he would draw them to him by the chains of his love."

The following St James' Day, after Holy Communion, our Lord made her perceive his presence in a quite extraordinary manner. She saw in front of her as it were a person who was wishing to conceal and to defend another, and at the same time he gave her a strong impression by which he let her know, that henceforth he would always be between her and all the mishaps which might possibly befall her, to hinder any reaching her. From that time she found herself so surrounded and shut up in the divine protection, that it seemed to her, she said, that Jesus and his holy Love had made themselves like strong walls to guard and defend her, and that she was shut up in God as in a tower or impenetrable fortress, where nothing whatsoever could find entrance to reach her ; and in truth all that since then might have been capable of touching or attacking her, was, as she saw, received by God himself, without her feeling anything of it any more than if she had lost her

being. Astonished at this, she used often say
to herself, " O poor Armelle, where art thou ?
Since the World, the Devil, or Sin, can no longer
find or reach thee." To which the divine impression made answer, " Thou are no more :
Thou art more lost in the ocean of my Divinity
than the fish is in the Sea."

Some time afterwards our Lord wished to
make known to what a point of purity and
cleanness his Love had brought her, and this he
did by showing himself as a person, who with a
lighted lamp searches in all the corners and
crannies of his house to see if he shall find anything which does not belong to him or which
is displeasing to him. Thus our Lord acted in
her soul, which was then established in a great
emptiness, and he let her know that he had not
found anything, and that there was none but
himself alone dwelling there. This almost
caused her to die on the spot from love and
gratitude to his divine Majesty, who had effected
in her such marvels.

In a conversation some days after the Festival
of the Conception of the Virgin, she said the
following words, " Since the Festival of my
holy Mother I have seen my soul detached from
all things, so pure, so disengaged, so single, that
it does not seem to me she inhabits my body,

which as if insensible merely follows her. I
have no longer any thought of anything which
arrests, or occupies me in the ordinary way.
There is one object alone, which is the Being
and Immensity of God, that penetrates and
consumes my soul in an inconceivable manner,
and while consuming, renders her of such vast
extent that I can perceive no bounds. Once
I wished to do everything, to embrace everything; but now it is not so; for nothing any
longer approaches me. I comprehend all and
am not comprehended of anything. My soul is
single, simple and pure, and when I see her thus
it is as a marvel. If this continues sometime
further in me I believe I must die. I go about
as usual in external matters without losing this
view; but my God takes it away sometimes
from me, permitting thoughts to pass through
my mind which divert me from it; otherwise
I should be dead already. The Love which
consumes me can be neither expressed nor conceived: it is as if infinite, and every day it still
further increases." These are her own words.

In this way she passed all Advent, still seeing
her soul removed and separate from her body,
and her body following it, like a valet, his master,
with such docility that it had not a movement
save for this alone; and her soul saw herself

led by the Spirit of God in a manner so clear
and evident, that she said, " The Spirit of God
animates my soul and gives her all the life and
movement that she has. His life is my life ;
his heart is my heart ; it is through him I
breathe and live."

CHAPTER XXI

THE first day of the year 1653 she failed not to ask her divine Love to give her a new year's gift, and addressing our Lord she said, " O my Love and my All ! you know it is usual with friends to give and ask from one another their new year's gift. I turn to you as my only and perfect friend, and I pray you give me for my present a great and living Faith and a constant presence of you, almost the same as with the Saints who see you in Heaven. For me, my Love, I can give you nothing ; for in vain I search within and without me, I find nothing that is not already yours. You have taken away everything from me, and you have not left me the least part that you have not taken and changed into you ; and thus I have no longer anything to give or offer you ; but as for you, give me, I pray, what I have asked." These words formed themselves in her spirit, without her having taken any care to arrange them so ; and she could not prevent herself uttering them, for, as we have often remarked, when God wished to bestow on her some signal grace, he usually

inspired her beforehand and urged her vehe-
mently, to make her ask it from him. This
she had constant experience of. From the
moment her prayer was finished God shed in
her soul a great light, and such an assured
and certain presence of his Majesty, that she
saw him as do the Saints in Heaven, which
cannot be better explained than in her own
words.

" I was," she said, " the first eight or ten days
of the year in a great assurance that my Love
and my All had granted me what I asked of him ;
for it is impossible to convey the clearness of the
faith he gave me of his divine presence. I saw
him clearly in my soul and all the operations his
divine Love was carrying on there. As for me,
I was steadfast, without movement and hardly
able to breathe ; I had no pulse ; in short, I
was dead to nature and lived the life of God,
attentive to see him, and to burn with a love
sweet and delectable, as the Saints burn in
Heaven. I had no thought of anything whatsoever, for God it was who thought and did
everything. In short, I cannot tell what, or
how, I was, except by saying that God alone
acted and effected everything ; and as for me, I
saw him clearly, and remained attentive and on
fire with a very great love, in a light which

seemed to surpass that of faith, so evident was
it, and which increased still more on the Day of
the Kings (Epiphany). During all this time I
was so feeble that I could scarcely move. I had
much difficulty in taking any food save the holy
Communion; not that I had any disgust, but I
was so full, soul and body, that this alone was
more than enough to sustain me. At first when
this took place I was exercised by great pains,
but these all went off; so that I kept saying to
myself, ' O, how true it is, that love is stronger
than all things ; for it absorbs and swallows up
all, and makes one feel and breathe only it alone.' "
Having in this state gone to see her Director,
she said to him after some discourse on the
mercies of God towards her, " Oh, my Father,
how willingly would I make the passage from
this life to the other I for it seems to me that
there is only half a step between me and it
already."

Some time after our Lord made her know, that
this passage had already been made, and that
she belonged no more to this world. He made her
understand, that if she was still of it, she could
not possibly have lived with the love, the purity
and innocence, in which she was living; and
that she saw it clearly by the continued view
she had of God, that there was no longer any-

thing between them both. This made her utter
with all the gratitude of her whole heart, " It is
true, my Lord, that you treat me as you treat
your Angels and your Saints, who see you incessantly. May your Holy Name be for ever
blessed." All this confirmed her in the certainty
she had, that God had granted her prayer, made
at the commencement of the year, to be always
in his divine presence. This view of God was
not merely at intervals and fleeting, but was
habitual. It was a firm and settled state, where
she seemed to be confirmed and established.
Therefore she said, " Nothing in the world can
thence withdraw my view : one could easier
hinder the flow and ebb of the tide than make
me turn my sight elsewhere."

Long before this, as we have already mentioned,
our Lord had opened the door of his divine heart
to her, to lodge her there, that it might be the
place of her dwelling ; but, on the eve of the
Presentation of our Lord in the Temple, he
wished to show her in a quite new fashion that
he had lodged her and introduced her into the
sacred Temple of his divine heart, and that she
was there in her own house. This is how she
described her state : " I found myself shut up
and lodged in the sacred heart of Jesus with
such love, glory, and freedom, that I could

not comprehend it. I was at large and
quite at my ease; nothing cramped me. I
saw this divine heart of such a vast extension
that thousands of entire worlds could not have
filled it.

I saw further that all those, who lodge within
through love, enjoy a true and entire liberty
and wonderful peace; on the other hand, I saw
that the door of entrance was so small and so
narrow that very few could find entrance there,
and surprised I said, "O my Love and my All,
how is it that your heart is large and spacious,
and one is so at large when within it, and yet the
door of entrance is so small and narrow? Then
our Lord made known to me, that it was because
he *wanted only the small, the naked, and the single
to be able to find entrance.* The *small* are those,
who with all the heart humble and abase themselves through love of him, these can enter;
the rest, not at all. For how could a person
swelled up with an esteem and opinion of himself
pass through such a small door? The *naked*
are those, who detach their heart from the
covetousness of the riches, and the comforts of
this life; for the rest, burdened with gold
and silver, or other things, it is impossible
to pass such a narrow place, until they have
got rid of their loads. The *single* are those

who detach their love from all creatures; for
love binds and attaches the heart to the thing
loved; and how can two bound together pass
where there is hardly room for one?

The days of the Carnival debaucheries approaching, she felt herself still more inflamed;
at which she was no wise astonished, for it was
usual with her to be so during those miserable
days, when most men forgot God; and as she
found herself so loaded with graces that she could
hardly keep up, she said to our Lord, " O my
divine Love, since all the world rejects you, this
is a good reason for you to keep to your friends,
and that they should aid you to carry your Cross
and the burden of the sins which are being committed. You so act with me, whom your Love
has made your friend and your bride.   You
lay on me great burdens; the one, from the
affliction and extreme pain I have at seeing you
offended; but the other utterly overwhelms me,
that is, the abundance of your graces.   It
seems, that all which the world rejects you
pour out in me; · since through your great
mercy you have made me a heart capable of all
which you will.   Blessed be your Holy Name for
ever !"

During these days of Carnival, being thus
occupied with her divine Love, she found her

heart one day so tender that she did nothing but weep, and knew not why ; for the ardour of the love which then occupied her was so great that it had taken out of sight and memory the offences against God and everything else. After she had much wept, and on recovering herself a little was seeking the cause, she found it was her divine Love who made her shed those tears for sinners, since he was no longer himself in a condition to do so.

On the first day of Lent there came to her a great desire to suffer something for her Love. Her desire was accomplished, but not in the ordinary way ; for God did not send suffering in the body. He permitted that, having a business to clear up with a person which closely concerned her, her mind insensibly dwelt an entire day in thinking from time to time of what had happened. On perceiving this she was much vexed to see that her understanding had been ever so little turned aside from God, so that she said the pain would have been insupportable had not God quickly applied the remedy. The following night she saw herself in the spirit introduced into the presence of the most Holy Trinity, as if she had been amidst the Courts of Angels, and the sight of God which she had previously had was still more clear than ever.

This made her say to our Lord, " O my dear Love, it seems that one had wished to draw a curtain between you and me to hinder me from seeing and contemplating you ; but your Love · could not suffer it. You have quickly removed it to make yourself still more clearly seen than I ever saw you before."

Afterwards, as she was thinking in herself whether anything would have been able to turn aside her look from such an amiable Object, and was resolving henceforth to avoid anything which could cause this evil, saying in the depth of her heart, " O never, my Love, no, never will I have to do with any one who can withdraw a thought from you, for I cannot pass a moment elsewhere." While in these holy affections, our Lord said to her, " that she was attached to the trunk of the tree of Life and that this tree is God ; and that, happen what might, nothing could ever detach her from it."

These last words produced a very great effect in her heart through the excessive love they kindled there, and for many days she seemed to hear continuously the voice of her Beloved, who kept saying to her the same thing. The desire then arose in her to ask him, " Why, my Love and my All, do you say that I am attached

to the trunk of the Tree of Life rather than
to the branches ? " " Because, my Daughter,"
answered our Lord, " thou art attached to Me
Alone, who am the trunk and the stem of eternal
life, and not to my gifts and my favours, which
are merely the branches that may be cut from it
and separated, with those who are attached
thereto ; but those who like thee are joined to
the trunk, seeking only Me Alone, shall never
be separated." These words well deserve the
attention of all those into whose hands it shall
please God that this writing fall.

It seems that our Lord made her hear them
only with a view to dispose her for the state
into which he brought her a few days afterwards,
to make her know, and those who directed her
conscience, that in truth she was attached only
to God alone, and not to the graces or extraordinary favours, which he had been wont to
confer on her every moment ; for after having
enjoyed for some time an ineffable love, the source
of which was in the divine Being, into whom God
made her know and feel that she was entirely
transformed, he suddenly withdrew her spirit
from the view of the operations he was carrying on in her soul, and left her as if naked
and despoiled of everything ; but nevertheless
in a manner so admirable that it merits well

to be recorded more at length in her own
words :

" I found myself," said she, " with respect to
my divine Love like a person who, after having
associated and conversed familiarly with his
intimate friend, seen and heard all his secrets,
and enjoyed fully the delight of his love, per-
ceives that his friend wishes to do something for
his good, of which, through an excess of goodness,
he is unwilling to give him the knowledge until
his design has been accomplished, and accordingly
keeps secret from him all that he is doing. This
is how I felt at the commencement of that state.
I knew that my only Love was enclosed in the
inmost of my soul and that he there was working
for his glory and my good ; but I knew not
what he was there doing ; my mind was at
the door of this sanctuary, without daring
or wishing to enter within. I was thus at
Easter and the week following, after which
I found myself so poor and so denuded of
everything that never had I been in such great
scarcity. Nothing any more occupied my mind,
either interior or exterior. It seemed to me
that I had no longer either faith, or love, or
attention to my God, save at intervals, and
rarely. I was a little surprised at this
novel state, without however wishing otherwise,

N

having through the mercy of God no other will
but his.

"After eight or ten days, when I went to
receive the holy Communion, my divine Love
made me understand that he had taken from me
everything I had, as they do to persons that are
declared spendthrifts, who are deprived of the
power of using their wealth. Then I said to
him, ' I am not astonished, my Love, that you
hide yourself from me, for when one is to be
declared spendthrift nothing is said to him until
the business is finished ; so have you acted in
my case, by rendering me poor, and despoiling
me of everything : Blessed for ever be your
Holy Name ! ' After these words I continued
as I was previously, and when I explained my
state to my Director, he told me that I had never
been better off than then, because all one can
see, receive, or experience, of God in this world,
is not purely God ; and that by this nudity and
poverty he was wishing to make a new approach
to my soul. They were such that I saw my
nothingness quite laid bare : my mind was very
free and nothing occupied it. Thus I continued
until the Ascension.

"On that day I felt in me two wills, the one was
that which through the mercy of God I have
always had, namely, of being very contented

with the state in which I found myself, wishing
nothing from Heaven or Earth but what I had
from moment to moment. But besides this
will, I felt another which watched for and desired
something new, and of this I tried to rid myself
as much as I could lest I should offend my divine
Love ; but the more I endeavoured the more
this will increased, and this made me believe
that it was without doubt the Holy Spirit who
was forming in me this desire, and thus I passed
the whole day ; but the thought occurred to me
that Love willed to confer on me some new
grace. The next morning at waking my mind
was raised to contemplate, as if without veil,
the glory which my Saviour enjoyed in Heaven
through his glorious Ascension. And I saw
that from his divine Heart issued forth a cord
of love and charity, which came to bind and
fasten mine so tightly, that the Heart of Jesus
and mine could never more be separated. I
could give no description of the love I then felt.
It was in no wise a human love, or which was
produced from me ; but it was the Charity of
God which overflowed in me. In this state I
communicated, without thinking on what I was
doing, my look being still engaged in Heaven. In
this state I continued until the following Sunday,
when going to receive the holy Communion, I

saw that the cord which kept my heart attached
gathered itself in and shut itself up in the Heart
of Jesus, and by this means it united and drew
together his and mine in a way that I cannot
explain.

" Thinking to myself of the great grace God
had bestowed on me through the merits of his
holy Ascension, he gave me to understand that
my divine love had treated me as he had done
the holy Apostles, from whom he had separated
himself as to corporal presence only in order to
give them a greater abundance of graces and
celestial consolations ; and considering how my
heart was thus bound to that of Jesus. Oh !
how I wished and desired that all the hearts of
men were thus bound and attached to that divine
Goodness, that they might never be able to
separate from it ! I passed several days in these
views and affections, after which I returned to
my former state, feeling only a holy and divine
flame, which is the pure love of my God, who
loves himself and has his pleasure in me, and
in loving himself in this way destroys me, consumes me, and reduces me wholly into himself
and makes my life to be more than human."

At the end of the Octave of the Assumption
of the most holy Virgin, our Lord according to
his custom willed to confer on his faithful servant

some signal favour, and as her soul had reached
an eminent degree of transformation into him,
as we have seen, his Majesty took pleasure in
making her understand it in a thousand ways
full of love and mysteries, which artlessly exhibited her state. Some days after the Festival
of the Holy Virgin he made himself seen and felt
in the inmost of her soul after the fashion of a
great sea, which had no bounds, and she delighted
herself and took her pleasure and her nourish-
ment in this Ocean, like a fish. Here are her
own words : " Being there," she said, " my Love
gave me to know, that as the fish cannot live
nor exist out of the water, so I could not live a
moment out of him, and as in whatever direction
the fish turns he always finds water, so in whatever place or manner I might be I should always
find him. I was nearly a month with this view,
at the end of which I lost the idea of the sea
and the fish to have only that of God alone, who
made himself perceived as shut up in the secrecy
of my soul, as her Conductor and Counsellor, so
that whatever offered itself to be done concerning either external or internal matters, I was
invited to enter into this secret cabinet to
receive orders on all I had to do or say, where
I was given a certain and assured light for
everything."

While all these operations passed in her soul her body was greatly weakened by the excess of divine love, but having been sent into the fields where she had many occupations, and being in need of strength and health to discharge them, our Lord gave it to her for the space of two months that her toil lasted.

CHAPTER XXII

IT was near Lent of the following year that her Beloved, filled with mercy and compassion for the loss of so many Souls redeemed by his precious blood, made her know, by a divine impression, that he wished her to employ herself to withdraw from sin these poor miserable sinners, saying to her in the inmost of her soul, " my beloved, thou art so won to Love that I leave thee in this world only for the purpose of drawing to it thy brothers, who estrange themselves from me by their sins : " and at the same moment he gave her such a lively feeling, at seeing her God so scorned by his creatures, and such a penetrating grief at their loss, that she could no longer doubt as to the sufferings with which our Lord willed to afflict her heart when he made her desire them so ardently at the commencement of the year.

" When," said she to me, " my soul was most sunk in the knowledge of the mercies of my God towards me, and my heart most on fire, or rather consumed by his divine Love, desiring with very great vehemence that all creatures should love him and praise him, it was then I knew more clearly than ever their ingratitude towards such an amiable Goodness and the blindness of the poor Souls, who turn aside from their sovereign good to cast themselves into an infinite unhappiness. Oh! how great and bitter were the distresses of my heart from these views, which daily increased to such excess that I lost all my strength! I could have wished to tear myself in pieces to repair the insults offered to Love. All I learned redoubled my pain; for he made me know that no one loved him purely, even among those who make profession of virtue; each one having his own ends and aims in scorn of his divine will."

" As for those who abandon themselves to vice, Good God! what knowledge have I not had of it! For very often it happened that persons with whom I had no acquaintance accosted me, to declare the terrible sins which were being committed, and in such secrecy, that I was surprised and startled how these things could be known; while they were told to me in all their circumstances. This pierced my heart with such extreme pain, that if my heart had been thrust through with a sword I could not have felt so much. I made my plaint to Love and asked why he permitted that I

should know these things; but he made me
understand ' *that, his goods being mine, his ills
must be mine also,*' which only still more tortured
me and increased the pain of my sufferings."

It was in truth worthy of admiration to see
the zeal of this holy woman to promote the glory
of God, in preventing through her prayers and
her energies that he should be offended. All
her thoughts, prayers, and actions had no other
end. She apparently forgot herself to think
only of the salvation of her neighbour. To hear
her one would have thought that she had to
render an account to God of each one. During
this time she knew persons of whom she had not
previously even heard. She prayed, and caused
others to pray, for the salvation of their souls,
and had no rest until she had endeavoured to
find some remedy for their irregularities. She
was so concerned for their misfortune as to
touch the hardest hearts.

Once a person unknown to her accosted her to
tell of infamous deeds that were being committed
in a certain house so secretly that, with the exception of the guilty, no one knew of them;
and as they were persons of rank it was a difficult
thing to find a remedy for these irregularities;
besides her condition as a servant much restrained her; but the love of God and the zeal

she had for the salvation of those persons, enabled her to find a means of withdrawing them from their sins and making them give up vice.

It was easy for those who knew her intimately to perceive when she had received similar news, for she was then so extraordinarily downcast that her life seemed at stake. I often questioned her when I saw her in this state, and it always turned out that some new offence had wounded her heart. When I enquired who had told it to her, she used to say, " I do not know, but it seems that Love wishes me to feel all his wounds, and that every one is hired to tell them to me."

One day when conversing with a great servant of God, who touched with the same sentiment at seeing him offended, was led to utter these words : " Let us quit, quit the earth, which is only sin and filth, and let us go to Heaven, where God is no more offended." She replied with an accent full of zeal, " What, my Father, is it thus you love your poor brethren ? Do you wish to leave them to perish in their miseries ? No, we must remain in this world to aid them to reach Heaven, that all together we may praise and bless Love." This was in truth her only employment, day and night. But to tell what passed between God and her is out of my power, for although she was always disturbed at the sins of her neighbours, this in no wise hindered the inconceivable joys she received from the sweet union of her soul with her Beloved, which she enjoyed to her heart's content in such a wonderful calm and tranquillity that one would have taken her rather for a soul of the Blessed than for one clothed still in mortal flesh. Her Saviour had in this made her like himself when he lived here below on earth, suffering in his soul an infinite grief at seeing his Father offended, and at the same time enjoying the immense delights of his union with the Divinity. This was the state she bore almost the entire year.

CHAPTER XXIII

In the month of October occurred a thing which will seem at first sight rather deserving of censure than of approval, particularly in a servant. It is, that many persons of virtue and merit had conceived so great an esteem for her saintliness, that they greatly wished to have her portrait taken, which was a genuine picture of modesty. They spoke to a painter, but he said he could not do it without her knowledge, nor unless she sat regularly for it.

Her Director at first feared to propose it to her, lest she should make a difficulty, but at last he spoke to her. She answered, " My Father, if you believe God will be glorified by it I am ready to do whatever you please."

The painter having set about taking her picture, Eternal Wisdom began to make another in the inmost of this Soul. " Having," she said, " withdrawn within myself, our Lord made me see the beauty with which my soul was adorned when regenerated by the waters of Baptism, pure, beautiful, without stain or defilement, but like a beautiful image made in resemblance of the

Divinity. Afterwards he made me see all my sins as stains which had spoiled, defiled, and defaced this beautiful image, so that no sign of its former beauty remained. At sight of this I conceived such grief at my offences that I knew not what to do. Tears flowed so abundantly that I was obliged to withdraw, telling the painter that I felt ill. This sight filled me the whole day; and the next day, the painter wishing to finish his picture, our Lord presented himself to my soul and showed me that from all eternity he had reserved her for himself, to paint there the infinite perfections of his Divinity, and that to efface the stains he had shed all his precious blood, which he had used as brilliant colours to embellish her; that she was a foundation on which divine Love, like a brush guided by the hand of his Wisdom, had never ceased working, and that at last he had rendered her so beautiful and so perfect that she was like to himself much more than she had been before I had spoiled her by my sins. O God! what love and what grief did my poor heart then feel! It was such that had not God supported me I had died on the spot."

Now while these admirable operations were taking place in her spirit, the painter was much hindered in finishing his work, and could not

succeed owing to the various changes he remarked in her face ; for he assured me he never
looked at her that he did not see her different,
at one time she was inflamed like a Seraph and
then pale as death, the eyes constantly filled with
tears—her appearance so sunk and absorbed,
with a modesty so divine, that it was impossible,
whatever trouble he took, to express with
his brush what the hand of God had imprinted
on her face.   His work was therefore poor
enough, and as he was ignorant of the cause of
these constant changes he attributed it to shyness
and shame at being looked at, so he only dared
to half look at her.   He was charmed and edified
by her modesty, and he told me he deemed
himself for ever fortunate in having seen this
holy woman, and that in his life he had never
observed such saintliness.

CHAPTER XXIV

ABOUT Christmas our Lord gave her such high notions of the admirable virtue of poverty, and so powerful a desire to practise it in the most eminent manner, that she burned with longing to bind herself to it by a vow. It is true that many years before she had felt this desire, but she had not then been able to effect it. The day assigned to make this vow of poverty was the first of the year 1655, but diverse causes delayed it until the Purification of the holy Virgin. As to the disposition of her soul after making this vow, here is what she subsequently declared to me :

" I would never have believed," said she, " that so many blessings were contained in the vow of poverty as my divine Love has made known to me, and although through his grace I was not attached to anything, I nevertheless cannot explain the freedom and detachment I find myself in ; having nothing now but pure Love, I am in a condition to no longer hope for anything but from him alone ; and since he has despoiled me of all, he has given himself entire

in exchange. You would have said he was only
waiting for this from me to make me enter into
participation of his divine plenitude. All he
had given me up to now appears nothing in
comparison with the profusion in which he now
communicates himself to my soul. It seems to
me that since the vow I made him my Love has
darted and cast himself into the inmost of my
soul and into all my powers, which he has so
abundantly filled with himself that I seem to be
already in glory."

She was in this state of plenitude of God for
more than a month after her vow, when it pleased
her divine Love to place her in a disposition quite
opposed to this, reducing her to a state of spiritual
poverty so great and so profound that she could
not make it understood or comprehended. It
was not a desertion, nor a dryness ; no, her state
was exalted above all that, and she made no
reflection on it ; for the union to which she had
attained permitted her to make no distinction
between the presence and absence of her Beloved.
The poverty to which she was reduced, being of
a nature quite different from what is ordinarily
understood under these terms, ought rather be
called an abundance of divine riches than a
want of them. " I find myself now through the
grace of my God," said she, " as poor interiorly

as exteriorly. My divine Love has despoiled
me of all : he no longer communicates himself,
nor flows into my soul or into any of my powers.
They are all free in their functions, and I can
apply myself with facility to everything which
has to be done, without any hindrance ; but he
has withdrawn into the centre of my soul, where
he governs and acts in me in a way I cannot
make intelligible."

Here we have the most usual state of her soul
since she made her vow, the first month excepted.
It is true that from time to time there occurred
something distinct, but very rarely. I can
only remember that, having seen her about the
Festival of the Ascension and found her extraordinarily moved by divine Love, I asked the
cause. She answered, that for some days her
mind was penetrated with grief for the sins of
men, and full of the desire to render to God,
according to her power, the honour of which
sinners deprived him by their sins, and after
shedding many tears she had fallen into a quite
mysterious sleep. In this she seemed to see a
person veiled like a nun, who, exhibiting excessive
grief at the offences committed against God,
urged her to feel them and to pray for the sinners,
and several times repeated to her these words:
" Let us love, let us love." " This person,"

o

she continued, "appeared to me so smitten with
divine love that I felt myself like ice alongside
her, and after she had many times said to me,
'Let us love,' she said, 'I give thee a share of
my Love,' and at the same moment I felt a love
so penetrating, so living, and surpassing so
strongly what I previously had, that I was near
dying from it. She disappeared at the same
time, and I was convinced it was the holy Virgin
who had bestowed that grace. When I awoke
from sleep I no longer knew myself, so ardent
and penetrating was the fire of divine Love,
and ever since I have been in the state you now
see me."

Our Lord, willing to call to him the mistress
of our good Armelle, sent her a very long and
troublesome illness, in which this faithful servant
rendered her all the services and assistance that
were possible, and with such assiduity, that
she did not leave her day or night except for
things absolutely necessary. As a consequence
she came very seldom to see me during the
eighteen months this illness lasted ; I can therefore not relate what passed in her soul until
after the death of her mistress, which took place
in October 1656. Having seen her some time
after, on my enquiries as to particulars of her
soul, she told me she had no idea of them,

as she was able to preserve none but that of pure Love, who most ordinarily kept her in the state of purity and poverty described before.

CHAPTER XXV

ALMOST all the time of her mistress's illness God had left the soul of this holy woman the free use of her faculties, without communicating to her any extraordinary grace, which might have hindered her rendering all the services she was required to her worthy mistress. This was the usual way God acted to her, as appears in this Life ; but on this occasion it was more apparent, as the period of time was much longer ; so that she believed the rest of her life would pass in this state, at which she was quite happy, since she therein saw the will of her Beloved. But very soon after the decease of her mistress she began to experience divine communications, which flowed through her soul with such impetuosity that they seemed to have been kept back and arrested by the circumstances mentioned.

He discovered to her then by a ray of his light the profound abyss of his infinite Goodness, Meekness, Peace and Tranquillity, as dwelling in the midst of his heart, and showed her that she possessed all these treasures in the depth of her soul. At the same time he made her feel, as far as she was capable, the same qualities which he showed to be in her, so that she seemed to have become all goodness, all peace, all meekness, all tranquillity. No other thought entered her mind and she could not even say any other word but this, "Goodness of my God! Meekness of my God! Peace of my God!" She would spend whole days repeating these words without tiring, and at night during her sleep she thought of nothing else in her dreams. On waking in the morning she found these words coming from her mouth, without any fixed intention, and her heart was as if drowned and submerged in the meekness and immense goodness of her God.

During this powerful experience, lasting over a month, she found herself so vigorous that she seemed to be in perfect health. "I was," said she, "so vigorous that I did not know myself; but it was a strength that was given me, to desire ardently that my Love should be loved and served by all his creatures. Oh! it seems to me, that were I allowed to cast into the hearts of men the least spark of the fire of holy Love which I feel, it would set them on fire, though they were ice! O infinite Goodness of my God, why are you so great in my case, and why do you not communicate yourself to others as well as to me, that all may be consumed by your Love ! O Meekness of my God, who can comprehend, who can conceive the close union that you have with your paltry creature ! "

For not more than a month she experienced this strength and vigour, after which she returned to her ordinary state of weakness and languor, but both alike caused by the divine operation. After having discovered to her his divine treasures which she held enclosed in her own breast, he showed her what she would be through all eternity. " For several days," she told me, " I seemed to see a great fire wherever I went, in which was a burning brand that this fire incessantly consumed, but which subsisted none the less ; and as I did not know what this meant, our Lord made known to me that this fire was none other than his Love, and that the brand was myself." When relating to me this remarkable favour, she was so exalted and so filled with love and gratitude for the bounties of God to her, that it seemed her heart would burst in pieces ; one would have thought her soul was about to leave her body. " O infinite Goodness of my God," said she, " how great is your Love towards your paltry creature ! Oh ! what a union you have made of a worm of the earth with your divine Majesty! Union which never is interrupted! Union which has made me like to you! for my love which is the bond of this union is a sharing in your infinite Love towards your creatures, and the sanctity which sanctifies me is a participation in yours. Oh! it is long since there has been either trouble or war in this poor heart because you govern it. In short, my God, I am no longer, but YOU ALONE; you live in me."

Her discourse was extremely long; this little will suffice to give some conception of the state of this great Soul, and I cannot omit what she further told me, that from the Festival of Christmas she saw that the eyes of her divine Love were unceasingly fixed upon her, and reciprocally they attracted those of her soul. It was in this mutual and divine regard that she passed almost the whole year. Her soul was so lost in this divine look that she did not understand it herself. She was as free to act in external matters as if nothing was taking place within her, and she had even good health so as to discharge all that was necessary of her house work. Thus she continued until the month of October, when constantly considering the goodness and perfections of her Beloved, her natural strength was extraordinarily reduced, and in a few days she was so weak that she could scarcely move. She was full and satiated with the goods of God which she had acquired by that divine look ; and she had such a disgust for all things of this world that, whatever effort she made, she could take no food but a few drops of broth.

Three weeks thus passed, when she had a strong wish to go and visit the tomb of St Vincent Fernier, Protector of that town to whom she had a special devotion. While there she felt such a powerful action of divine Love, and her strength so weakened that she thought her last hour had come, and leaning as best she could against the wall, she said to our Lord : " My Love, if it was your Will, I should be very happy to die in this place, but if it is not your good pleasure, finish what is so far advanced." Wonderful instance of the goodness of God towards his faithful servant ! She had hardly finished her prayer when she found herself as strong, as sound, as active as ever, and her appetite as good as when in the best health. This was a new ground for her loving her Benefactor, and for thinking that he willed still to leave her in this world to burn and consume with his Love.

CHAPTER XXVI

A PRAYER which she had often made during her life was in part granted, and from Ascension Day of the year 1658 she passed almost the rest of her days without God communicating to her anything of an extraordinary nature ; not that he had deserted her, but he worked in the depth of her soul in so divine and exalted a manner that she herself did not comprehend it, and could give no account thereof. Here is what she one day said to her Director and to me, who had several times enquired about the state of her interior disposition, " My Father," speaking to her Director, " I believe that my Love and my All has at last heard the prayer I so often made, that he would deprive me of all his graces and favours in order to give them to those who knew him not, that by this means they might be led to love him with all the heart ; and that I would willingly deprive myself of every good in order that my God should be loved by a single Soul. He knows that I have never desired anything but himself alone, and now he gives himself to me in that way. He is enclosed in this poor heart which he governs as God. I am quite certain he is there. Oh ! what peace and what tranquillity reigns there ! No : there is no longer anything in this poor heart save GOD QUITE ALONE, and this is Life Eternal."

Then addressing herself to her divine Love, she said to him, " O my Love and my All ! who could ever have thought to see this heart in the state in which it is ? O Love ! although you are always the same, yet how different you are in your operations, and how well you know how to accommodate yourself to our weaknesses ! Where is the time, O divine Love ! when you acted in this heart as Conqueror and Vanquisher, armed with fire and flames, burning, setting fire to, consuming everything that opposed itself to your divine volitions, penetrating it with your darts and your arrows, so that each day I expected to die ? And you never left it at rest until you had conquered and triumphed. Afterwards, O divine Love, you reigned there as King, peaceful and powerful ; as Father, very gentle and pitiful ; and as Spouse, full of love and liberal, distributing to it your graces and your favours with an excess that you alone know, O divine Love ! And now you reign there as God. Yes : my God, you are there, quite such as you are, incomprehensible and inaccessible,

Armelle Nicolas

in this poor heart that you so guard that nothing approaches it but YOU ALONE."

From these words one may judge of the interior state of this great Soul in her latter years, during which God communicated himself to her as God. It is not that sometimes she did not feel the flames of his divine Love, more quick and penetrating at one time than another; but, as it was without any intermediary, she could not make it understood. She had then always this presence of God in the manner described. As to her exterior, everything was quite ordinary, showing nothing else but an eminent sanctity in all her actions. Her health was fairly good, with freedom and presence of mind to discharge the duties of her station, until it pleased our Lord to deprive her of it by an accident.

CHAPTER XXVII

BEFORE concluding this narrative I will give a few extracts taken from the second Part of the original Life which illustrate the saintliness of its subject and the perfection of Divine Love manifested in her.

" Never," she used to say, " had I asked anything so much of my divine Love as this ardent prayer which I made to him every day, that of his divine mercy it would please him to place me among the number of his Disciples and give me admittance to his School and make me a servant in his Holy House and receive me into his Company as he had done his Apostles and Disciples. Alas ! when I made these prayers with so much fervour that often I was beside myself, I did not know, nor understand, what I was saying. But, O my God, how well I afterwards understood the sense of my words and how you have accomplished my requests ; for by your great mercy you have received me into your School and you have admitted me to your Company, where I, poor ignorant that I am, have learned more in one day than all men together could have taught me in my whole life.

" After God had showed me this favour, to make me always feel his presence, and he was pleased to undertake my conducting, I abandoned myself entirely to him ; so that I no longer considered myself but as the Disciple of God and Schoolgirl of the Holy Spirit. I was always attentive in myself to love him and to consider what he commanded me, to carry it out ; and when anything arose to be done, I behaved exactly as a servant or Disciple does to his master's order. In doing it I had my view directed upon him, to imitate what he had done in this world ; and if it was a thing which he had not done, he taught me the manner of accomplishing it in the way most agreeable to him.

" Thus in all things great and small he instructed me, and not only he instructed me, but he himself by an excess of goodness governed me, and sometimes he made me understand that I was like those little scholars who commence learning to write, to whom the master is not satisfied with giving an example or a model, but himself takes the hand of the pupil and guides it, in order to teach him thus to form his letters. I was exactly the same in regard to God, and often I felt as if another hand guided

mine. This was no matter of the imagination
or fancy, but the genuine and pure truth, which
I saw more clearly than the day."

" In all circumstances I had recourse to my
God with more freedom than a beloved child
has to his father, who idolizes him. I conversed
confidentially with him. I told him all my
troubles, all my wants and needs. I consoled
myself with him. I rejoiced at his divine perfections. I asked him what was needed for me
and for my neighbours, whom I regarded as my
own brothers. If I wished to treat with him
as with my intimate Friend, he listened to me
and treated me in this relation, communicating
to me his secrets, as two friends do, one to the
other. If I addressed myself to him as a poor
Disciple, rude and ignorant, he instructed me
in my doubts, enlightened me in my obscurities,
encouraged me in my weaknesses, corrected
and reproved me with love and strictness in
my faults, teaching me himself the fashion and
manner in which I ought to perform my actions ;
making me in all things know that which was
best, to follow it, and that which was bad, to
avoid it.

" If my love led me to consider him as my
Spouse, it was here he made me sensible of the
greatest endearments and favours ; which were

such as would pass for incredible to any one who
had not experienced them. Then he gave himself
entirely to me, as I gave myself entirely to him ;
then he made me understand that he was wholly
mine ; then he caressed me, united me and
transformed me ; and that at every hour, every
moment, without anything in the world being
able to separate me from him, caressing me so
tenderly that I was forced to say to him that
I could endure no more, and that'if he continued
he would cause me to die. At other times I
used to say to him that it seemed he had nothing
else to do but to caress and console me ; and
sometimes the force of this same love drew from
my mouth these words, ' Ah, my dear Love !
if the world knew the tenderness you every
moment make me experience, it would say that
the love you bear me is excessive ; and if I
dared, I would say it myself.' "

On the Day of Conversion of St Paul 1643,
she was awaked by hearing herself called in a
loud voice, which she mistook at first for that of
her fellow-servant, who, however, had not done
so. At the end of a week, as she thought with
herself what it could mean, she was told interiorly
that by this God called her to an entire fidelity.
She then asked, " What is Fidelity ? " The
answer was, " It is to do perfectly as well small

things as great ; for Fidelity is that which unites the soul to God, and infidelity separates us."

In her low origin and condition of a servant she found motive of unceasing thankfulness to God. "When I consider," she used to say, "the good fortune of my condition and the great advantages therein, I can never weary of blessing my divine Love for having placed me in it, and I find nothing in the world more desirable, nor which ought to be more esteemed and cherished, than this ; for it is a place where one has to live continually despised by every one : who could make count of a poor servant ? Every one has power to reprove and despise her, and to find fault with all she does or says. Does not this teach one to keep humble, to put one's reliance and confidence in God, and to seek only to please him ? Therefore often I have been astonished to see poor girls complain and afflict themselves at what should rejoice and console them. O poor creatures ! I used to say to myself, if you knew the great good there is in being despised, chidden and ill-treated, you would feel joy in place of the sadness which gnaws you."

When urged to give up her occupation as a servant to embrace a life offering, as was thought, greater scope for spiritual contemplation, she

said, that her work and her occupation did not
hinder her from enjoying God ; on the contrary,
she had remarked that the more she worked and
employed herself for her Love in all the worries
of housework, the more he communicated himself
to her ; that she would commit a great infidelity
to leave her work for rest ; that God knows how
to find souls everywhere, provided the entrance
of the heart is not closed against him.

" And the idea that a mean servant, a poor
village girl, a worm of the earth like me, should
have pride ! One must be mad to come to that,
or else not know what I know. If God has
had pity on me ; if he has deigned to undertake
himself the troubles of instructing, of teaching
me, of giving me lights and knowledge that poor
peasants such as I do not ordinarily possess :
if he has forestalled me with his graces, burnt
and consumed me with his divine Love ; it has
been his goodness and mercy alone that have
done all that ; not I, nor any of my good works.
For if God treated me according to them, he
would give me no other place in Hell but under
the feet of Lucifer, being the place I deserve.
But his great mercy makes me hope he will treat
me not according to my works, but according
to his goodness." . . .

" The more my divine Love caressed me, the

P

more I saw my baseness and my nothingness ;
so that often I was as if astonished and beside
myself that such high Majesty should be willing
thus to communicate himself to a poor servant ;
and sometimes I said to myself, Were it not that
I well know my Love sees and knows all, I would
think that he does not see my abjectness.   Often
also these views were taken away, for the force
of love raised me above myself and prevented
me dwelling on myself or anything which concerned me, and when I had told my Confessors
the great graces shown me, I lost all recollection
of them, Love so powerfully occupied me that
nothing remained to me save HE ALONE."

In the outflowings of Divine Charity which
filled her she thus interceded for those who
neglected and despised God's light. " I wept
their faults with continued tears, and I had my
heart so full of tenderness and compassion for
them that I felt their sufferings more than my
own. Love furnished me with a thousand
inventions to excuse them to God. I cried
incessantly for mercy on them. Day and night
I cast myself at his sacred feet to obtain their
pardon.   I said to him that they were his
children, that they had cost the blood of his Son
and that for his love he must save them, that
they were poor blind ones, who knew not what

they were doing ; that if they had known, they never would have offended him ; that in short they were my brothers, whose loss I could not endure, and that I felt it as my own ; and the Goodness of my God was so great towards me that he made me know, that since they were my brothers he would have pity on them. What an excess of Goodness ! therefore since then I give them hardly any name but that of ' My brothers.' It seems that when I have said to him ' My Love and my All ! they are my brothers : pardon them ; have mercy on them '; I have nothing more to say to recommend them and to obtain his pity for them : so excessive was his love towards his. poor servant."

Of poverty of spirit she thus spoke :—

" Oh ! happy those who abandon everything ! for they will find all ; but we must abandon even up to the least part of ourselves ; not only in what we see to be bad, but further in what we believe to be good. For God never will reign in us until we shall have entirely given ourselves up to him and allow him to do in us what to him seems good, without our troubling ourselves at what he shall do, or allow to be done. Therefore since he has made me know him so clearly as I know him, I let him do all he pleases. If he makes himself seen and felt by me, I let him

p*

do so. If he keeps hidden and concealed, I do not ask to see him. In short, he is master and king of my heart. There he has established his reign and is there so absolute that I sometimes say to him, that it seems to me he will not be more so in Heaven."

" He has taken from me everything and he has given me Himself, and having him I esteem myself more rich than if I possessed all the riches of Heaven and earth. I am but a poor village girl, but in my poverty I possess all good, all peace, all joy, all contentment, because I have my God, who is my All ; and in possessing him, all that is his is mine ; as all that there was of me is now by his grace all his."

Here is a description of her Daily Practice :—

" It seemed that I was the child of Love and that he was my Father and my Guide, who led me as if by the hand to all I had to do : and as for me, I had no other care but to look at him and do what he commanded me without ever departing therefrom. He taught me to regard him so continually that from morning to night I had no other object in my thoughts, and if at times I was in the least diverted, immediately I placed myself again in his divine Presence and there I worked to please him alone. I conversed with him during my work. I loved him

and rejoiced in him. I treated with him as
with my most intimate friend, and if occupations called me, which required all my attention,
I had, however, my heart always turned to him,
and when they were finished I ran to him again,
exactly as does a person who passionately loves
another : whatever business he has he only
half leaves him. I was exactly the same with
my God, from whom it was impossible for me
to separate and I could live only in his presence ;
for I knew well and he himself taught me, that as
long as I kept my look on him I could not offend
him or prevent myself from loving him."

" The more I looked at him, the more I knew
his divine perfections and my nothingness and
wretchedness ; so that I forgot myself, and
abandoned myself as a thing unworthy of thought
to rise above myself and all created things, to unite
and attach myself incessantly to him. All my end
was to please him in what I did and to watch
against offending him. In all my actions I thought
of nothing else. This I did not for the benefit
that might accrue to me, nor to avoid the ill
which would have followed my doing otherwise ;
all these views and interests were so remote
from my mind that I never thought of them.
Love alone carried off everything for him, and
provided he was content, I was satisfied."

" As to my daily practices, they were just
as I have said. On my first awaking I threw
myself into the arms of my Divine Love, as a
child does into those of his father. I got up to
serve him and to work, in order to please him.
If I had time to pray, I placed myself on my
knees in his divine Presence and spoke to him
as if I saw him with my eyes. There I offered
myself entirely to him. I prayed him that in
me might be accomplished all his holy wills,
and that he would not permit me to offend him
in the slightest thing. Moreover I offered to
him all the Masses that during the day would be
said throughout Christendom, and prayed him
to apply their merits for relief of souls in
Purgatory. In short, I occupied myself in him
and his praises as often as my work allowed me ;
but generally I had not time to say a *Pater* or
an *Ave* during the whole day. But I did not
in the least trouble myself at it. It was as
much to my heart to work for him as to pray to
him ; because he had taught me that whatever
is done for his love is a true prayer."

" I dressed myself in his company, and he
showed me that his love furnished me with
clothing. When I was at my work, he did not
leave me, nor did I quit him. He worked with
me and I with him ; I was always as united

and attached to him as when at prayer. Oh !
how sweet and easy to bear were all my troubles
in such good company ! Therefore I drew from
it such strength and courage that nothing was
hard to me, and I would have liked by myself
to have done the whole work of the household.
I had only my body at work ; the heart and all
myself burned with love in the sweet familiarity
I had with him. If I took my food, it was in
his divine Presence, as well as all the rest, and
it seemed to me that every morsel was soaked
in his precious Blood, and that he himself gave
it to nourish me, that I might burn still more
from his love."

" If in the course of the day, amidst bother
and continual occupations, the body felt fatigue
and would have liked to complain, murmur,
take its ease, or let itself be carried away to
anger or some other movement of disorderly
passion, immediately Love enlightened me and
showed me that I ought to kill these rebellions
of nature and not encourage them by word or
action. He was as the gatekeeper of my mouth
and a guard to my heart, that nothing might
contribute to nourish these irregular movements,
and thus they were constrained to die at their
birth. If at times I was not sufficiently upon
my guard, and allowed myself to be carried away

by surprise to some fault, I could not endure
until I had obtained my pardon and peace was
made between him and me. I wept at his sacred
feet and told him my fault as if he had not seen
it ; I confessed my weakness to him and could
not stir from there until he had pardoned me,
and friendship was become stronger than ever,
which through his goodness and mercy happened
all the times I fell into faults ; and this only
served to burn me still more with his divine Love.
When men persecuted me by their slanders and
ill-treatment, and the devils in their temptations
and vain artifices, at the same moment I turned
to my Love, and he stretched his sacred arms
to me and showed me his Heart and his wounds
open, to lodge me within and keep me safe.
Therefore I thrust myself in there as into my
true Fortress, and there I was stronger than all
Hell ; and though all creatures had risen up
against me I would have had no more fear of
them than of a fly ; for I was under the safe
guard and protection of Love."

"If at times he himself left me and made a
show of withdrawing, I used to say, 'Oh ! it does
not matter, my Love ; it is idle for you to conceal
yourself. I will not the less serve you ; for I
know that you are my God.' And then I tried
to keep more on my guard than ever and to be

more faithful, lest I should displease my Love ; for that was my only apprehension. During those times I recognised more my paltriness and my poverty, and I trusted myself more to our Lord, being content to be in that state all my life, if it was his pleasure. But he hardly left me in it at all ; if I dared say so, I would say, that he could not prevent himself from caressing me, any more than I could live without him. For in requital for one moment of absence, on his return he loaded me with so many graces, such tender and divine favours that I could not support them ; and often I was constrained to cry that I could stand no more, and that he should moderate them, or I would die under the burden of his graces. It was vain for me to cry out to him, that it was not his caresses and his graces I asked, but HIM ALONE without other things. I had to suffer and support them since such was his holy Will."

Much more follows of the same character relating to her attendance at Mass and Confession and other religious ceremonies.

" Such has been the life of a poor peasant, and a mean servant since Love divine had been willing to undertake her guidance. Here is how he drew me from the misery of my sins and ignorance to make me what I am through his

great mercy ! ! Such is the life I led for twenty
years, without ever feeling the least diminution
of the love he poured into my heart from the
moment of my entire conversion !

" It is in his infinite Love I find myself satiated
and satisfied, and until I reached this my soul
always was a-hungry, though it seemed to me I
could not have more than what I had at each
moment. Now I did not reach this until by his
great goodness it pleased him to introduce me
into his house. (See Chap. xv.) I had for
twenty years," said she, "lodged in my own,
leading the life I have just described. But after
that time he made me enter into his ; which is
nothing else but HIMSELF. Since that time
what passes in me is so exalted above all that
there was previously, that it is impossible to
make it understood. The creature seems to be
there entirely lost. The spirit is so raised above
the earth that it does not seem to be on it. The
peace is so profound, the joy so perfected, that
the soul thinks herself already entered into the
peace and joy of God—transformed into God."

On the 10th August 1671 Armelle was attacked
by severe fever, which, after abating somewhat
in severity, ultimately carried her off on the
24th October following. The whole town was
concerned at the news of her illness, and numbers

filled the room of the dying woman on the last days. Her master ordered that her body should be treated with the same honour as if she was his own daughter, and when it lay covered in white with the funeral candles around, he came with uncovered head, knelt at the foot and kissed the bare feet. All his family and many other persons did the same.

According to her desire the body was buried in the Chapel of the Ursuline Convent in front of the Grand Altar though the Chapter desired to have it buried within the Cathedral. The heart enclosed in lead was taken as a relic by the Jesuit College, one of the members of which composed for her tomb the following Epitaph.

HERE LIES THE BODY OF
ARMELLE NICOLAS
A PEASANT BY BIRTH ; BY OCCUPATION A SERVANT,
COMMONLY CALLED
THE GOOD ARMELLE
AND IN THE INEFFABLE COMMUNICATIONS
SHE HAD WITH GOD
THE DAUGHTER OF LOVE.
SHE DIED ON EARTH TO LIVE IN HEAVEN
THE 24TH OCTOBER 1671 AGED 65 YEARS
PRAY FOR HER SOUL AND WALK IN HER STEPS
BY LOVING GOD AS SHE DID.
REQUIESCAT IN PACE
AMEN

CATALOGUE
OF PUBLICATIONS
AND
IMPORTATIONS OF

All Books are Cloth Bound, except where otherwise stated, and may be had of all Booksellers, or will be sent to any part of the world on receipt of price and postage. **All** previous Catalogues are hereby cancelled. All prices net.

H. R. ALLENSON, LIMITED
RACQUET COURT, FLEET STREET
LONDON, E.C.

À KEMPIS. THE IMITATION OF CHRIST. Edition of 1633. Demy 16mo, cloth, 2s. 6d. net; by post 2s. 9d.

ALEXANDER. THE GLORY IN THE GREY. Talks on Life and Religion. By the Rev. ARCHIBALD ALEXANDER, M.A., B.D. 3s 6d. net; by post 3s. 11d.

Dr GEO. H. MORRISON writes :—" Its freshness, variety, suggestiveness, and poetry have fascinated me. It seems to me one of the best things of the kind I have read for years. I have found it a little haven of rest in these troublous times."

—— A DAY AT A TIME. Talks on Life and Religion. By the Rev. ARCHIBALD ALEXANDER, M.A., B.D. 2s. 6d. net; by post 2s. 10d.

The Rev. JOHN KELMAN, D.D., writes :—" I find it everywhere an excellently timely and helpful volume. It is the sort of book which is needed during these dark days by large numbers of people, and it will do real service to the spirit of the nation."

ALLENSON. THOUGHTS WORTH THINKING. A Day-Book of Encouragement and Cheer. Compiled by H. R. ALLENSON. Cloth, 1s. net; art paper sides, 1s. net; leather, gilt edges, 2s. net; leather, round corners, 2s. 6d. net; persian velvet, gilt edges, 3s. 6d. net; postage 2d. extra. [*Third Edition.*
DUNDEE ADVERTISER.—" The quotations will give impetus to the best that is in every reader, and provide a measure of encouragement to him to face the difficulties of life in a cheerful spirit. A pleasant volume to send a friend as a reminder of good fellowship."

ANDERSON. LARGER THAN THE CLOUD. A Sequence of Sermons in War Time. By the Rev. H. R. ANDERSON, M.A. 2s. net; by post 2s. 4d.

ALLEN. ARMELLE NICOLAS. By T. T. ALLEN, with Introduction by Prof. DOWDEN. 5s. net. Translation from the French.

A Great Classic of the Devotional Life.

ANDREWES. PRIVATE DEVOTIONS. Entirely new reprint of Newman and Neale's translation. Demy 16mo, 2s. 6d. net; by post 2s. 9d.
CHURCH TIMES.—" As neat and handy an edition as any with which we are acquainted."

—— BISHOP ANDREWES' PRIVATE DEVOTIONS. Dean Stanhope's Translation. [See Sanctuary Booklets.
Dr ALEX. WHYTE writes :—" Circulate it with all your might."

AUSTIN. SEEDS AND SAPLINGS. 105 Original Outline Sermons. By the Rev. F. J. AUSTIN. 1s. net.
THE CHRISTIAN.—" A compendium that will be of much practical utility."

BAILEY. THE NIGHT WIND, AND OTHER POEMS. By H. I. S. BAILEY. Paper wrapper, 1s. 6d. net.

BANKS. COMMON-SENSE TALKS ON HEALTH AND TEMPERANCE. By A. M. BANKS. 1s. net; postage 2d.
Speakers to men and women will here find much valuable material.

BERNARD. RHYTHM OF BERNARD OF MORLAIX. Original text and translation by J. M. NEALE. [See Sanctuary Booklets.

BOEHME. THE SUPERSENSUAL LIFE. By JACOB BOEHME. [See Heart and Life Booklets.

BOILEAU. THOUGHTS FOR CHRISTIAN WOMEN. By the late
M. G. BOILEAU. 1s. net.
Practical outlines of Biblical Teaching on Eating and Drinking, Dress, Recreation, Work,
etc. Topics of real service to Speakers.

BONAR. HYMNS OF FAITH AND HOPE. By HORATIUS BONAR,
D.D. [See Heart and Life Booklets.

BONAVENTURA. THE GOLDEN ALPHABET OF SAINT BONA-
VENTURA. [See Sanctuary Booklets.

BROOKS. LECTURES ON PREACHING. By PHILLIPS BROOKS, D.D.
2s. 6d. net; postage 4d. extra.
———— THE INFLUENCE OF JESUS. By Bishop PHILLIPS BROOKS,
D.D. 2s. 6d. net; post free 2s. 10d.
———— LETTERS OF TRAVEL (1865-1890). By Bishop PHILLIPS BROOKS.
2s. 6d. net; postage 4d. extra. Bishop Brooks' personal life.
———— THE PURPOSE AND USE OF COMFORT. A Sermon.
[See Heart and Life Booklets.
———— AN EASTER SERMON (Rev. i. 17 and 18).
[See Heart and Life Booklets.
———— THE LIFE WITH GOD. Addressed to business men.
Fourth Edition. [See Heart and Life Booklets.

BROWN, R. M. FORTY BIBLE LESSONS AND FORTY ILLUS-
TRATIVE STORIES: (THE BIBLE IN LESSON AND STORY). By R. M. BROWN. 3s. 6d.
net; by post 3s. 11d.

BROWNING, ROBERT. EASTER DAY.
———— CHRISTMAS EVE.
———— SAUL. [See Heart and Life Booklets.

BURN, MARY. GATHERED ROSEMARY, from GEORGE HERBERT'S
POEMS. [See Heart and Life Booklets.

BUSHNELL. THE CHARACTER OF JESUS. By HORACE BUSHNELL,
D.D. [See Sanctuary Booklets.

BUTCHER. TO BOYS: TALKS ON PARADE. By the Rev. J. WILLIAMS
BUTCHER. 2s. 6d. net; by post 2s. 10d.
BRITISH WEEKLY.—"Extremely attractive addresses. The book sparkles with virile and
racy anecdotes."

CAIRD. RELIGION IN COMMON LIFE. By Principal JOHN CAIRD,
D.D., LL.D. [See Heart and Life Booklets.

CAMERON. CHRIST IN DAILY LIFE.
———— SAINT PAUL IN DAILY LIFE. Daily Readings from the Gospels,
Acts, and Epistles. By ADELAIDE M. CAMERON. 2 vols. Cloth, 1s. net; leather, 2s. net;
velvet calf, 3s. 6d. net each.
———— THEIR WEDDING DAY, and other Stories. By ADELAIDE M.
CAMERON. Handsome cloth, cr. 8vo. 1s. 6d. net.
CHURCH TIMES.—"Just the thing for Mothers' Meetings, will be enjoyed for their insight
into human nature."

CARLYLE. HEROES AND HERO WORSHIP. India Paper, 516 pages,
limp leather, 1s. 6d. net; postage 2d.
The most perfect pocket edition extant.
———— HEROES AND HERO WORSHIP. Paper, 6d. net.
———— SARTOR RESARTUS. Paper, 6d. net.

BOYD-CARPENTER. THOUGHTS ON PRAYER. By Bishop BOYD-
CARPENTER. Cloth, 1s. net; leather, 2s. net; postage 2d.
———— FOOTPRINTS OF THE SAVIOUR. By Bishop BOYD-CARPENTER,
D.D. Thirteen illustrations. 2s. 6d. net.

CARTER. VOICES OF THE PRAYER BOOK. Lectures on the Prayer
Book, etc. By the late Mrs E. C. CARTER, St Jude's, Whitechapel. Cloth, 1s. net;
paper, 6d. net; postage 1d.

CAWS. THE UNFOLDING DAWN. Sermons by the Rev. LUTHER W.
CAWS. 3s. 6d. net.

CHAMBERS. LETTERS ON MARRIAGE. By Mrs CHAMBERS. 1s.
net; postage 2d.
Recommended by the Dowager Countess of Chichester, the Lady Betty Balfour, Mrs
Creighton, and Mrs Maude.

CHILD. ROOT PRINCIPLES IN RATIONAL AND SPIRITUAL THINGS. By THOMAS CHILD. 164 pages, paper, 6d.; cloth, 1s. net; postage 2d.

CHURCH. THE GIFTS OF CIVILISATION. By DEAN CHURCH, M.A. Paper, 6d.; by post 8d.
The BISHOP OF LONDON says :—"I am very glad that Mr Allenson is issuing a cheap edition of this beautiful book."

CLARKE, E. A. L. THE PEOPLE'S MISSAL. Compiled by the Rev. E. A. L. CLARKE, A.K.C. 508 pages. Fcap. 8vo. Cloth, 3s. 6d. net ;'leather, 5s. net and 6s. 6d. net ; postage 4d. extra.

CLARKE, W. N. HUXLEY AND PHILLIPS BROOKS. By Prof. W. NEWTON CLARKE, D.D. *Fourth Edition.* Postage 1d. [See Heart and Life Booklets.

COLEY. NATURE TALKS FOR PRIMARY WORKERS. By Miss MAY COLEY. 1s. net.

COMPTON. TRUE ILLUSTRATIONS FROM THE WAR. Compiled by the Rev. J. E. COMPTON. 1s. net ; by post 1s. 2d.

COOTE. THOUGHTS ON MOTHERHOOD. From MANY MINDS. Compiled by Lady COOTE of Ballyfin. 192 pages, leather, gilt edges, 2s. net ; postage 2d.
A most charming gift-book of choice and happy pieces.

CRAKE. THE TRAGEDY OF THE DACRES. By the Rev. E. E. CRAKE, M.A. Illustrated. 2s. 6d. net ; by post 2s. 11d.
A fine historical romance.

CRITCHLEY. THE LEGEND OF THE SILVER CUP, and other Allegories for Children. By the Rev. GEO. W. CRITCHLEY, B.A. Illustrated. Third Edition. 2s. 6d. net : by post 2s. 10d.

DAILY MESSAGE FROM MANY MINDS, A. India paper. Velvet persian, 3s. 6d. net ; by post 2d. extra.
Also in demy 16mo, 2s. 6d. net ; Leather, 2s. 6d. net ; by post 2s. 9d.
BOOKMAN.—"A particularly well chosen day-book of beautiful verses and prose passages. Ranges from cheery practical encouragement to high ideals."

DALE. RELIGION : ITS PLACE AND POWER. By the Rev. H. MONTAGUE DALE, M.A., B.D. 3s. 6d. net ; by post 3s. 9d.

DARWIN. MY GERMAN PROFESSOR : A true Story of Yesterday and To-day. By Mrs M. D. DARWIN. Paper, 1s. net ; by post 1s. 2d.

Fine Manual for Christian Workers.

DAVEY. METHODS OF CHRISTIAN WORK. Hints for Preachers, Teachers, and Lay Workers. By the Bishop of SALISBURY, Bishop THORNTON, Prebendary CARLILE, and other Workers of the Church Army. With Foreword by the Bishop of LONDON. Edited by Captain W. R. DAVEY. 1s. 6d. net : by post 1s. 9d.

DEATH AND LIFE. Letters from the Correspondence of a Parish Priest. 2s. 6d. net ; by post 2s. 10d.

DINWOODIE. ILLUSTRATED SERMON OUTLINES. By J. DINWOODIE. 2s. 6d. net; by post 2s. 10d.
SCOTSMAN.—"To the young cleric and the lay preacher on the look-out for the groundwork for the composition of sermons, Mr Dinwoodie's book should prove a valuable acquisition."

DOLE. THE RELIGION OF A GENTLEMAN. By C. F. DOLE, D.D. Second Edition. 3s. 6d. net.
PUBLIC OPINION.—"Remarkably suggestive."
——— THE THEOLOGY OF CIVILISATION. By CHARLES F. DOLE, D.D. Second Edition. 3s. 6d. net.
EXPOSITORY TIMES.—"It is full of new thoughts."
——— THE COMING PEOPLE. A Study of Life in its Social and Religious Aspects. By C. F. DOLE, D.D. Fifth Edition. 3s. 6d. net.
METHODIST RECORDER.—"Distinctly refreshing."
THE SPECTATOR.—"Healthy and virile."

DOWSETT. WITH GOD AMONG THE FLOWERS. Fifty-two Addresses to Children. By the Rev. L. E. DOWSETT. 2s. 6d. net.
——— WITH GOD IN MY GARDEN. Fifty-two Talks to Children. By the Rev. L. E. DOWSETT. Second Edition. 2s. 6d. net ; by post 2s. 10d.
These strikingly fresh books supply a long-expressed want for suggestions for addresses for Flower Services.
YORKSHIRE OBSERVER.—"It would be difficult to imagine a series of more delightful talks. The lessons are wrapped up in the story in such a way that the lesson becomes the delightful thing."

DRUMMOND. PARABLES AND PICTURES FOR PREACHERS AND
TEACHERS. Compiled by the Rev. J. S. DRUMMOND. 2s. 6d. net.
Capital collection of anecdotes and illustrations.

DUFF. ILLUMINATIVE FLASHES. Compiled by JAMES DUFF. 1s. net.
New Collection of 300 very useful illustrations.

EAMES. THE SHATTERED TEMPLE. Addresses to Young People.
By JOHN EAMES, M.A. 1s. 6d. net; by post 3s. 11d.
——— SERMONS TO BOYS AND GIRLS. By JOHN EAMES, M.A.
Third Edition. 1s. 6d. net; postage 3d.
METHODIST TIMES.—"Examples of what children's addresses ought to be—simple in
language, but pointed in teaching."

ECKHART. SERMONS BY MEISTER ECKHART.
[See Heart and Life Booklets.

EDDISON. TALES THE OLD GOVERNESS TOLD. By AMY G.
EDDISON. 2s. 6d. net; by post 2s. 10d.

EDWARDS. TIN TACKS FOR TINY FOLKS. Outline Addresses, in-
cluding Twelve Addresses on Birds. By Rev. C. EDWARDS. Fourth Edition. 2s. 6d. net.
METHODIST TIMES.—"A mine of thought and illustration."
——— TIN TACKS FOR TINY FOLKS. By Rev. C. EDWARDS. Fourth
Edition. 1s. 6d. net.
Without the twelve Bird chapters.
——— A BOX OF NAILS FOR BUSY CHRISTIAN WORKERS. By
Rev. C. EDWARDS. Ninth Thousand. 1s. 6d. net.
CHRISTIAN.—"The pages abound in material for evangelists and other workers, sound in
substance and direct in aim."

ELLIS. OUTLINES AND ILLUSTRATIONS. For Preachers, Teachers,
and Christian Workers. Comprising 600 Outlines of Addresses, Bible Readings, and
Sunday School Talks, together with over 250 Illustrations and Incidents. Compiled by
J. ELLIS. Being "Tool Basket," "Seed Basket," "Illustrations and Incidents," bound
in one volume. 2s. 6d. net; by post 2s. 10d.
THE CHRISTIAN.—"Here is the scaffolding on which to build hundreds of addresses."
——— EVANGELIST'S WALLET FOR PREACHERS, TEACHERS,
AND CHRISTIAN WORKERS. Outlines of Addresses by J. ELLIS. Thirteenth
Thousand. 1s. net.
LOCAL PREACHER.—"Brimful of excellent suggestive outline addresses."
——— THE PREACHER'S AND TEACHER'S VADE-MECUM. Being
"Evangelist's Wallet," "Outline Sermonettes," and "By Way of Illustration," in one
volume. 2s. 6d. net; by post 2s. 10d.
DAILY NEWS.—"It might be called 'Preaching made easy.'"
——— TOOL BASKET FOR PREACHERS. 300 Outline Addresses.
Compiled by J. ELLIS. Forty-fifth Thousand. 1s. net.
——— SEED BASKET FOR MINISTERS. 300 Outlines. By J. ELLIS.
Thirty-fifth Thousand. 1s. net.
PRIMITIVE METHODIST.—"Three hundred excellent outlines."
——— ILLUSTRATIONS AND INCIDENTS. For Preachers, Teachers,
and Christian Workers. 250 Anecdotes and Facts. Thirtieth Thousand. 1s. net.
——— BY WAY OF ILLUSTRATION. Thirteenth Thousand. 1s. net.
Collection of Illustrations for Public Speakers.
LOCAL PREACHERS' MAGAZINE.—"Wonderfully fresh; one of the very best compilations
of the kind that we have seen."
——— TOOLS FOR THE MASTER'S WORK. 250 Sermon Outlines
and Children's Addresses. Collected by J. ELLIS. Third Edition. Crown 8vo. 1s. 6d. net.
METHODIST TIMES.—"Another valuable volume. Just the suggestions and hints we so
often want."

ELLIS, J. J. PLUCK, PATIENCE, AND POWER: The Life Story of
JOHN PEARCE, Founder of "Pearce and Plenty." By J. J. ELLIS. 1s. 6d. net; by post
1s. 10d.
A stirring story of self-help. "A sensible book to put into the hands of lads who have any
grit in them."

EMERSON. ENGLISH TRAITS. By R. W. EMERSON. Paper, 6d. net;
by post 8d.

ENTWISTLE. OUTLINE MISSIONARY TALKS AND STORIES. By
EMILY E. ENTWISTLE. 1s. net; postage 2d.

EVANS. A PRIMER OF FREE CHURCH HISTORY. By A. JOHNSON EVANS., M. A. Paper, 6d. net; postage 2d. Recommended by Dr CLIFFORD.

FABER. SELECTION FROM F. W. FABER'S HYMNS.
Twelve of Faber's beautiful hymns, each complete. [See Heart and Life Booklets.

——— WISHES ABOUT DEATH. Fifteen More Hymns from F. W. FABER. [See Heart and Life Booklets.

FÉNELON. THE MAXIMS OF THE SAINTS. By ARCHBISHOP FÉNELON. [See Heart and Life Booklets.

——— MEDITATIONS FOR A MONTH. By ARCHBISHOP FÉNELON. [See Heart and Life Booklets.

FOX. SEVEN VISIONS OF THE COMING CHRIST. Reprinted from "Rays of the Dawn," by RACHEL J. Fox. Cr. 8vo, Art Paper, 1s. net; by post 1s. 2d.

FREETH. THE TRUE THEOLOGY. By J. T. FREETH. A Reply to R. J. CAMPBELL. Paper, 6d.; by post 8d.

GILLIE. WHAT I SAID TO THE CHILDREN. By Rev. R. C. GILLIE, M.A. 1s. net.

——— LITTLE SERMONS TO THE CHILDREN. By Rev. R. C. GILLIE, M.A. 1s. net.

——— LITTLE TALKS ON TEMPERANCE. By the Rev. R. C. GILLIE, M.A. 1s. net.

GLEDHILL. A PACKET OF SUNLIGHT. By the Rev. MORTON GLEDHILL. 1s. 6d. net; by post 1s. 9d.
Twenty-six Talks to Children, full of striking illustrations.

GREENWELL. CARMINA CRUCIS. 3s. 6d. net. Reprint of very scarce volume of poems by DORA GREENWELL, with an Introduction by Miss C. L. MAYNARD. SCOTSMAN.—" Among the best religious poetry of the nineteenth century."

——— SELECTED POEMS FROM DORA GREENWELL. Chosen and edited, with Introductions, by Miss C. L. MAYNARD. 3s. 6d. net.
NEWCASTLE DAILY CHRONICLE.—" Many will find comfort and consolation in these earnest and beautiful poems."

——— EVERLASTING LOVE AND OTHER SONGS OF SALVATION. [See Heart and Life Booklets.
DUNDEE ADVERTISER.—" No more useful religious writing has been done than these pieces describing the practical application of faith to the lives of the simple and the partially educated."

GREGORY. AN INTRODUCTION TO CHRISTIAN MYSTICISM. By ELEANOR C. GREGORY. [See Heart and Life Booklets.

——— THE UPWARD WAY. Readings for one month from SAMUEL RUTHERFORD. Compiled by Miss E. C. GREGORY. [See Heart and Life Booklets.

GREGORY, SAMUEL. AMONG THE ROSES. Twenty-nine Addresses to Children. By Rev. SAMUEL GREGORY. 342 pages. 3s. 6d. net; by post 3s. 11d.

GUYON. LIFE OF MADAME. New ed. 6s. net. [See Upham.

——— SPIRITUAL TORRENTS. By MADAME GUYON. 2s. 6d. net; postage 4d.

——— A SHORT AND EASY METHOD OF PRAYER. By MADAME GUYON. [See Heart and Life Booklets.

HALL. THE SINNER'S FRIEND. By J. V. HALL. 6d. net; 1s. net; 2s. net; postage 1d. [See Heart and Life Booklets.

HAMILTON. THE WONDERFUL RIVER. Sixty-three Talks to Young People. By Rev. JOHN A. HAMILTON. 3s. 6d. net.
BRITISH WEEKLY.—" This writer is a true story-teller. These attractive addresses will be most acceptable to children and teachers."

HAMPDEN. THE CHANGED CROSS. By the Honble. Mrs HOBART HAMPDEN. [See Sanctuary Booklets.

HANDLEY. WHAT ENGLAND OWES TO THE PURITANS. By Rev. S. B. HANDLEY. Paper, 6d. net; post free 7d.

HARVIE. THE KING'S UNIFORM. Addresses to Children. By the Rev. ROBERT HARVIE, M.A. 1s. net; postage 2d.
Illustrations are most convincing. For those who have felt a difficulty in telling children about the war, this book should be an inspiration how to do it.

Strikingly Fresh Addresses to Children.

HASTIE. UNDER THE BLUE DOME. Open-Air Studies with Young Folk. By Rev. J. S. HASTIE, B.D. 3s. 6d. net.
S. S. CHRONICLE.—" As a sanctified study of nature it is one of the freshest books of its kind we have seen for a long time."

LARGE TYPE.   PRETTY GIFTS.

" Attractive little Reprints of Great Utterances."

THE HEART AND LIFE BOOKLETS

Two-Coloured Printed Wrappers, 6d. net; Handsome Cloth Gilt, 1s. net; Choice Leather Gilt, 2s. net. Postage One Penny each.

THE LONELINESS AND SINLESSNESS OF CHRIST. By F. W. ROBERTSON. Two of his most famous sermons.

THE PURPOSE AND USE OF COMFORT. By PHILLIPS BROOKS, D.D. A fine piece of consolation in time of trouble from loss by death.

AN EASTER SERMON. By PHILLIPS BROOKS, D.D. A cheering message of hope.

SELECTIONS FROM FABER'S HYMNS. Twelve beautiful expressions. Each complete.

THE LIFE WITH GOD. By PHILLIPS BROOKS, D.D. A specimen of Brooks's magnificent eloquence, originally delivered to business men.

HUXLEY AND PHILLIPS BROOKS. By W. N. CLARKE, D.D. A powerful and sympathetic piece of criticism.

EASTER DAY. By ROBERT BROWNING. Fine presentment of this famous religious poem.

RELIGION IN COMMON LIFE. By JOHN CAIRD, D.D., LL.D. Dean Stanley—"The greatest sermon in the language."

CHRISTMAS EVE. By ROBERT BROWNING. One of the most popular of Browning's poems.

AN INTRODUCTION TO CHRISTIAN MYSTICISM. By Miss GREGORY.

THE MYSTERY OF PAIN. By JAMES HINTON.

A PSALTER FOR DAILY USE. Selected by Professor WILLIAM KNIGHT, LL.D.

EVERLASTING LOVE. Songs of Salvation. By DORA GREENWELL. Fragrant with the true devotional spirit.

THE PRACTICE OF THE PRESENCE OF GOD. Conversations and Sixteen Letters of Brother Lawrence. Sweet, simple, and practical.

THE SPIRITUAL MAXIMS OF BROTHER LAWRENCE. No edition since 1741.

THE DREAM OF GERONTIUS. By CARDINAL NEWMAN. One of the most original poems of the 19th century.

A SHORT AND EASY METHOD OF PRAYER. By MADAME GUYON. Fénelon helped to circulate this book.

THE SUPERSENSUAL LIFE. By JACOB BOEHME. First cheap issue of this work of the great German mystic.

MEDITATIONS FOR A MONTH. By ARCHBISHOP FÉNELON. A most interesting introduction to this most famous French divine.

MAXIMS OF THE SAINTS. By ARCHBISHOP FÉNELON. A translation of his celebrated work on the love of God.

THE UPWARD WAY. Readings for thirty-one days from SAMUEL RUTHERFORD. Selected and arranged by Miss GREGORY.

HYMNS OF FAITH AND HOPE. By HORATIUS BONAR. Choice selection.

MEISTER ECKHART'S SERMONS. Translated by Rev. CLAUD FIELD, M.A. ST PAUL. By FREDERIC W. H. MYERS.

THE WAY OF VICTORY. By Miss JEAN ROBERTS. With Introduction by the Abbot of Caldey.

THE LITTLE FLOWERS OF ST FRANCIS OF ASSISI. First twenty chapters.

THE SPIRITUAL GUIDE. By MIGUEL DE MOLINOS. Compiled and Edited by Rev. Canon R. Y. LYNN.

SAUL. By ROBERT BROWNING. A fine printing of one of Browning's noblest poems.

THE SINNER'S FRIEND. By J. V. HALL. Nearly three millions have been sold of this book in tract form. It is here finely presented in a permanent binding.

GATHERED ROSEMARY. FROM GEORGE HERBERT'S POEMS. Edited by MARY BURN. Introduction by Bishop of Hull.

THE SPIRIT IS LIFE. Selections from the letters of WM. LAW.

WISHES ABOUT DEATH. Fifteen More Hymns from F. W. FABER.

THE COMRADE IN WHITE.

BY THE REV. W. H. LEATHEM, M.A.

DUNDEE COURIER.—"Every household that has one or more of its members at the war should possess itself of 'The Comrade in White.' There is something in it for them more precious than fine gold."

HILTON. AN IMAGINATIVE CHILD. Studies from a Child's Point of View. By Miss AGNES A. HILTON. 1s. 6d. net.
Fine Study of Child Life.

HINTON. THE MYSTERY OF PAIN. By JAMES HINTON.
[See Heart and Life Booklets.

HOARE. THE WORKER'S BIRTHDAY BOOK. Compiled by Miss
O. HOARE. Two pages to a day. 750 pp. Cloth, 2s. net; leather, 3s. 6d. net; Persian
mor., 5s. net.
A unique book. Containing Prayer for each day, Scripture text and prose, or poetical
extract and room for Birthday names and other events.

HORNE. THE PRIMER OF CHURCH FELLOWSHIP. By Rev. W.
PIERCE and Rev. C. S. HORNE, M.A. Sixth Edition. Cloth, 1s. net; paper wrapper, 6d.

HORTON. THE INVISIBLE SHIELD, and other Parables. By Rev.
SAMUEL HORTON. 2s. 6d. net; by post 2s. 10d.
Striking parables which will be most useful as illustrations.

JACK. AFTER HIS LIKENESS. Addresses to Young Men and Women.
By J. W. JACK, M.A. Cloth, 3s. 6d. net.

JARVIS. THREE GIRLS AND A GARDEN, and other Stories. By
M. R. JARVIS. 2s. 6d. net; postage 4d.
"It is just the thing for a young women's class or a mothers' meeting, and if read once will
be asked for again. Every story is splendid."

————— PLEASING STORIES FOR MOTHERS' MEETINGS AND GIRLS'
CLUBS. By M. R. JARVIS. 1s. 6d. net.

————— KINDHEARTED STORIES FOR MOTHERS' MEETINGS AND
GIRLS' CLUBS. By M. R. JARVIS. 1s. 6d. net.
The above two titles represent a reissue in separate volumes of Mrs Jarvis's book, "Three
Girls and a Garden," hitherto a single volume. The stories are all of an uplifting and en-
couraging character.

————— REST AWHILE STORIES. By MARY ROWLES JARVIS. 1s. 6d.
net; postage 3d.
Dr CAMPBELL MORGAN.—"A capital volume. I do not know a better collection for
reading in Mothers' Meetings or similar gatherings."

JOHNSON. PRAYERS AND MEDITATIONS. By Dr SAMUEL JOHNSON.
2s. 6d. net; by post 2s. 9d.
CHURCH TIMES.—"There was no greater man in the eighteenth century than Dr Johnson.
He was a downright Church of England man."

JOWETT. BROOKS BY THE TRAVELLER'S WAY. Twenty-six
Week-night Addresses. By J. H. JOWETT, M.A., D.D. 2s. 6d. net. Fourth Edition
(Eighth Thousand).

————— THIRSTING FOR THE SPRINGS. By the Rev. J. H. JOWETT.
Twenty-six Addresses. 2s. 6d. net. Seventh Thousand.

KEBLE. THE CHRISTIAN YEAR. By the Rev. JOHN KEBLE. 2s. 6d. net.
THE SATURDAY REVIEW.—"A very dainty edition."

KEEP. OLD TESTAMENT LESSONS. Delivered to a Girls' Bible Class.
By Miss M. I. KEEP. 3s. 6d. net.

KNIGHT, Prof. WM. A PSALTER FOR DAILY USE.
[See Heart and Life Booklets.

LAMOREAUX. THE UNFOLDING LIFE. A Study of Development
with Reference to Religious Training. By A. A. LAMOREAUX. 1s. net; by post 1s. 2d.

LAW. A SERIOUS CALL TO A DEVOUT AND HOLY LIFE. By
WILLIAM LAW. 188 pages, paper, 6d.; cloth, 1s. net; postage 3d.
The BISHOP OF OXFORD says.—"Law's 'Serious Call' is an admirable book, of the pro-
foundest piety. May I venture to suggest to the clergy that they should both read it themselves and make a serious effort to promote the study of it in their parishes."

LAWRENCE. THE PRACTICE OF THE PRESENCE OF GOD. By
BROTHER LAWRENCE. Sixteen Letters. [See Heart and Life Booklets.
Also 32 mo, cloth, 6d. net; leather, 1s. net; velvet calf, 1s. 6d. net.
[See The Sanctuary Booklets.
These editions of the Conversations and Letters contain an additional Letter never before
included in English issues. Insist on Allenson's Edition.

————— SPIRITUAL MAXIMS OF BROTHER LAWRENCE, and his
Character and Gathered Thoughts. [See Heart and Life Booklets.

LEADER. FOLLOW THE CHRIST. Talks to Boys on the Life of
Christ. By the Rev. G. C. LEADER. 2s. 6d. net; by post 2s. 10d.
LIFE OF FAITH.—"Mr Leader has achieved a real success. Preachers and teachers will be
greatly enriched through the study of this book."

————— WANTED—A BOY. Addresses to Children. By the Rev. G. C.
LEADER. 1s. 6d. net; by post 1s. 9d.
LIFE OF FAITH.—"This is a manly book for manly boys."

LEARMOUNT. THE YEAR ROUND. Fifty-two Talks to Young Folk,
By J. LEARMOUNT. 3s. 6d. net ; by post 3s. 11d.
" Crooked Joe," one of its many stories, deserves telling to every Boys' Club or class.

——— GOD'S OUT-OF-DOORS. Fifty-two Talks on Nature Topics.
3s. 6d. net ; by post 3s. 11d.

——— IN GOD'S ORCHARD. Addresses to Children. 3s. 6d. net ; by
post 3s. 11d.

——— FIFTY-TWO SUNDAYS WITH THE CHILDREN. 3s. 6d. net ;
by post 3s. 11d.
BRITISH WEEKLY.—" Brightened with many telling illustrations, well adapted to their
purpose."

——— FIFTY-TWO ADDRESSES TO YOUNG FOLK. By Rev. JAMES
LEARMOUNT. Fifth Edition. 3s. 6d. net ; by post 3s. 11d.
This volume contains " The Third Finger."

LEATHEM. THE HOUSE WITH THE TWO GARDENS. Twenty-two
Parables and Addresses to Children. By the Rev. WILLIAM H. LEATHEM, B.D. 1s. net ;
by post 1s. 2d.

The Wounded and the War.

——— THE COMRADE IN WHITE. By the Rev. W. H. LEATHEM,
M.A. [See Heart and Life Booklets.
CONTENTS.—1. In the Trenches. 2. The Messenger. 3. Maimed or Perfected. 4. The
Prayer Circle.
Dr F. B. MEYER writes :—" The booklet brought a mist over my eyes. It is well worth
reading, and wherever it is read it will help."

LEWIS. THE MAGIC PEN. Story Addresses for Children. By E. W.
LEWIS, M.A. 2s. 6d. net.
MORNING RAYS.—" Nothing less than perfectly delightful."

——— SOME VIEWS OF MODERN THEOLOGY. Sixteen Sermons on
Vital Questions. By the Rev. E. W. LEWIS, M.A. Second Edition. 3s. 6d. net.

——— CONCERNING THE LAST THINGS. Sunday afternoon Sermons
to Men. By the Rev. E. W. LEWIS, M.A. 1s. net ; by post 1s. 2d.
Five addresses on Death, Judgment, Heaven, Hell, The Coming of Christ.

LIDDON. CHRIST'S CONQUEST, and other Sermons. By Rev. CANON
H. P. LIDDON. Paper, 6d. ; by post 8d.

LILY. JACK THE FIRE DOG. By AUNT LILY. 2s. 6d. net ; by post
2s. 11d. Illustrated.
The life story of a dog attached to a Fire Station.

LITTLE. THE OUTLOOK OF THE SOUL. Twelve Sermons by CANON
KNOX LITTLE. 356 pages, 2s. 6d. net.

LIVES I HAVE KNOWN. With an Introduction by the BISHOP OF
DURHAM. 1s. net ; post free 1s. 2d.
JOYFUL NEWS.—" Ten stories of lives saved and kept to the end. Simply told with a
natural charm which makes them strong evidence of the power of God to save from all sin."

LOVE. TALKS TO CHILDREN. By Rev. J. LANDELS LOVE. 1s. 6d.
net ; by post 1s. 9d.
These twenty-five Talks are good. Mr Love catches the attention immediately and holds it,
and he has always a good illustration at command.

Three Great Classics of the Devotional Life.

MACDUFF. THE BOW IN THE CLOUD. Words of Comfort for Hours
of Sorrow. By Dr J. R. MACDUFF.

——— THE MORNING WATCHES. By Dr J. R. MACDUFF.

——— THE NIGHT WATCHES. By Dr J. R. MACDUFF.
[See Sanctuary Booklets.

MACFADYEN. CONSTRUCTIVE CONGREGATIONAL IDEALS.
Cheap edition. 1s. net ; postage 4d.

MACLEAN. THE SECRET OF THE STREAM. By the Rev. J. B.
MACLEAN, B D. 2s. 6d. net ; by post 2s. 10d.
GLASGOW HERALD.—" Fresh, thoughtful, and suggestive, Mr Maclean writes sermons which
are good to read."

MACLEOD. THE GOLD THREAD. By NORMAN MACLEOD. 1s. 6d net.
Contains all the original full-page illustrations.
S.S. MAGAZINE.—"A beautiful allegory of the Gospel, and ought to be put in the hands of every young person. This book ought never to be omitted in choosing prizes."

M'WILLIAM. SPEAKERS FOR GOD. Plain Lectures on the Minor Prophets. By Rev. T. M'WILLIAM, M.A. 3s. 6d. net.

MACY. SOME MISTAKES OF THE HIGHER CRITICS. By S. B. MACY. Seven full-page illustrations. 1s. net.
The BISHOP OF BRISTOL.—"Concise, pointed, accurate, and very effective."

MARSHALL. HOMELY TALKS WITH MOTHERS. Twenty-four Addresses by Mrs L. C. E. MARSHALL. 1s. net.
The BISHOP OF ELY says:—"Models of what Addresses to Mothers should be—simple, practical, earnest, devout, brightened by touches of poetry and humour."

——— BREAD FROM HEAVEN. Addresses to Communicants. By LUCY C. E. MARSHALL. 6d. net.
FRIENDLY WORK.—"Giving full and careful teaching."

MARTIN. GREAT MOTTOES WITH GREAT LESSONS. Talks to Children on Mottoes of Great Families, etc. By the Rev. G. CURRIE MARTIN, M.A. 3s. 6d. net.
SPECTATOR.—"In this volume we have a good idea well executed."

MARTIN. A CATECHISM ON THE TEACHING OF JESUS. By Rev. G. CURRIE MARTIN, M.A., B.D. For use in Schools and Bible Classes. Third Edition 16 pages, stout wrapper, 1d. ; cloth, 2d. ; postage ½d.
Rev. Dr CLIFFORD.—"This Catechism is one of the best I have seen."

——— OUTLINE SERMONETTES ON GOLDEN TEXTS. Edited by Rev. G. CURRIE MARTIN, M.A. Fourth Edition. 1s. net.
SUNDAY SCHOOL CHRONICLE.—"Rich in thought, and exceedingly suggestive."

MARTIN, LUCY. ECHOES OF HELP AND COMFORT. Collected by LUCY E. MARTIN. Cloth, 3s. 6d. net ; by post 3s. 9d.

MARTINEAU. ENDEAVOURS AFTER THE CHRISTIAN LIFE. By JAMES MARTINEAU. Two Series complete in one vol., 335 pages. 1s. 6d. net ; by post 1s. 10d.
Separately First and Second Series, paper, 6d. net each ; by post 8d. each.
THE BAPTIST TIMES.—"These famous sermons are among the very greatest of the Victorian era. In this well-printed edition we can purchase them for a tenth of their original cost."

——— WHAT IS CHRISTIANITY ? Being a Reprint of "The Rationale of Religious Enquiry ; or, The Question stated by Reason, the Bible, and the Church." By JAMES MARTINEAU. Paper, 6d. net ; by post 8d.

MARZIALS. IN THE LAND OF NURSERY RHYME. By Miss ADA M. MARZIALS. Frontis by BYAM SHAW. Third Edition. 2s. net ; by post 2s. 3d.
Mr GEO. H. ARCHIBALD writes:—"I like these stories very much. The morals are exquisitely buried."

——— MORE TALES IN THE LAND OF NURSERY RHYME. By Miss ADA M. MARZIALS. 2s. net ; by post 2s. 3d.

M'CONNELL. WHITE WINGS. Seventeen Addresses to Young People. By the Rev. THOMAS M'CONNELL, B.A. 1s. net ; by post 1s. 2d.

MATHEWS. BATTLE AND VICTORY. By Mrs W. G. MATHEWS. 1s. net.
Capital reading book for Mothers' Meetings and Working Parties.
Very Suitable for Recitation.

MAYNARD. WATCHING THE WAR. A Chronicle of Successive Events. By C. L. MAYNARD. Four Parts. Paper, 6d. net each ; cloth, 1s. net each.
The BISHOP OF DURHAM writes :—"With my whole heart I bid God-speed to 'Watching the War.' I have read it from cover to cover, and the impression of its splendid worth has seemed to grow with every page ; certainly with every chief poem."

MILLER. PORTRAITS OF WOMEN OF THE BIBLE. Vol. I., Old Testament ; Vol. II., New Testament. By the Rev. T. E. MILLER, M.A., Dunfermline. 3s. 6d. net each.
ABERDEEN FREE PRESS.—"Must have been good to hear, for they are good to read."

MILLARD. THE QUEST OF THE INFINITE ; or, The Place of Reason and Mystery in Religious Experience. By BENJAMIN A. MILLARD. 2s. 6d. net.

MOLINOS. THE SPIRITUAL GUIDE. By MIGUEL DE MOLINOS. Edited by Canon R. Y. LYNN. [See Heart and Life Booklets.

MOMERIE. IMMORTALITY AND OTHER SERMONS. By Prof. A. W. MOMERIE, M.A., LL.D. Fourth Edition. 3s. 6d. net.

———— IMMORTALITY. Thirty-five Chapters. By Prof. A. W. MOMERIE, M.A., LL.D. Popular Edition, Thirty-fifth Thousand. Paper, 6d. net ; by post 8d.

———— PERSONALITY. By Prof. A. W. MOMERIE. Paper, 6d. net ; by post 8d.

———— INSPIRATION. By Prof. A. W. MOMERIE. Paper, 6d. net ; by post 8d.

———— BELIEF IN GOD. By Prof. A. W. MOMERIE, M.A. Second Edition. Paper, 6d. net ; by post 8d.

———— THE ORIGIN OF EVIL, and other Sermons. By Prof. A. W. MOMERIE. Ninth and cheaper edition. Paper, 6d. net ; by post 8d.

MOORE. MAN PREPARING FOR OTHER WORLDS. By Rev. W. T. MOORE, M.A., LL.D. 508 pages, 2s. 6d. net ; by post 2s. 10d. EXPOSITORY TIMES.—"A delight to read."

MORROW. QUESTIONS ASKED AND ANSWERED BY OUR LORD. By the Rev H. W. MORROW, M.A. 3s. 6d. net.

MOULE. MEDITATIONS FOR THE CHURCH'S YEAR. By the Right Rev. H. C. G. MOULE, D.D., Bishop of Durham. 2s. 6d. net. THE CHRISTIAN.—"Dr Moule at his best."

MYERS. SAINT PAUL. By F. W. H. MYERS. Demy 16mo, handmade paper, cloth, or leather, 2s. 6d. net. Dr J. H. JOWETT writes :—"Exceedingly beautiful copy. I think it is most admirably done."

———— SAINT PAUL. By FREDERIC W. H. MYERS. 6d., 1s., and 2s. net. [See Heart and Life Booklets. Also miniature vest pocket edition, 6d. net, 1s. net, 1s. 6d. net. [See The Sanctuary Booklets.

NANKIVELL. A SCHEME OF TEACHING FOR THE CHURCH'S YEAR ; and a Year's Course of Lessons for Sunday-School Classes. By C. NANKIVELL. 2s. 6d. net ; by post 2s. 10d. THE CHURCH TIMES.—"The educated Churchman who is called upon to instruct the young, be he priest or the youngest of Sunday-school teachers, will find it most useful. The freshness of the book makes it essentially superior to others of a similar kind."

NEALE. SACKVILLE COLLEGE SERMONS. By the late Rev. J. M. NEALE, D.D. 2s. 6d. net ; by post 2s. 11d. Vol. I.—Thirty-one Sermons, Advent to Lent. Famous Sermons, long out of print. THE CHURCH TIMES.—"We can never have too much of Dr Neale. Gladly, therefore, do we welcome a reprint of the Sackville College Sermons. Neale is never old-fashioned, for it is the eternal truth of God that he has ever to tell us."

———— SERMONS ON THE BLESSED SACRAMENT. Twenty-two Sermons. By the late J. M. NEALE. 2s. 6d. net. Uniform with "Sackville College Sermons."

———— SERMONS FOR CHILDREN. Thirty-three Addresses. By the late J. M. NEALE. 2s. 6d. net.

———— THE RHYTHM OF BERNARD OF MORLAIX. Translated by J. M. NEALE. [See Sanctuary Booklets.

NEWMAN. TWELVE SERMONS. By J. H. NEWMAN. Paper, 6d. net ; by post 8d. "The finest sermons ever preached from the Anglican pulpit."

———— THE DREAM OF GERONTIUS. By Cardinal NEWMAN. [See Heart and Life Booklets and The Sanctuary Booklets.

———— BISHOP ANDREWES' DEVOTIONS. Translated by J. M. NEALE and J. H. NEWMAN. 2s. 6d. net ; by post 2s. 9d.

NICHOLSON. THE WONDERFUL CITY. Twenty-six Addresses to Children. By Rev. CECIL NICHOLSON. 1s. net; post free 1s. 2d.

THE NONCONFORMIST MINISTER'S ORDINAL. Preacher's Services for Baptismal, Dedication, Marriage, and Funeral Services. Large type. 1s. net; postage 2d.
This book will go comfortably into a breast pocket.
LITERARY WORLD.—"A work many Nonconformist ministers will be glad to know of. As convenient in size, type, and binding as could well be."

NORTHCROFT. FORCES THAT HELP. By FLORENCE NORTHCROFT. 1s. 6d. net; by post 1s. 9d.
METHODIST TIMES.—"Those who speak at mothers' meetings will find help here."

OMAR KHAYYAM. FITZGERALD'S TRANSLATION. Leather, gilt edges, 1s. net; cloth, gilt, 6d. net.
Very dainty reprint of SECOND edition (110 stanzas), with variations of FIRST edition at end. There is more of Fitzgerald's work in this little book than in any other cheap edition. 28 illustrations.

PALMER. THE GOSPEL PROBLEMS AND THEIR SOLUTION. By JOSEPH PALMER. 6s. net.

PALMER, Mrs. MOTHERS' UNION WORK—A VOCATION. By Mrs T. F. PALMER. 1s. net.

PARKER, A. S. WINNING THE CHILDREN. Story Addresses. By the Rev. A. STANLEY PARKER. 1s. 6d. net.

PARKER. JOB'S COMFORTERS; or, SCIENTIFIC SYMPATHY. By Rev. JOSEPH PARKER, D.D. Paper, 6d. net.
In the form of a parable; many very brilliant passages of dialogue.
W. E. GLADSTONE.—"A Satire which Dean Swift would have admired."

———— GAMBLING. By JOSEPH PARKER, D.D. Paper, 3d. net; post free 3½d. Fifth Edition.
METHODIST TIMES.—"We hope this mighty address will stir the heart of England and awaken the conscience of the nation."

PARKINS. BUSINESS LIFE. By W. J. PARKINS, Director and Secretary of Tangye's Ltd., Birmingham. 1s. net.
ENGINEERING.—"The business world would be the better if this advice were taken to heart, not alone by the office boy, but by those above him."

PERREN. REVIVAL SERMONS IN OUTLINE. Edited by Rev. C. H. PERREN, D.D. In Two Parts. Part I., Methods; Part II., Outlines of Sermons and Addresses. Complete in one volume. 344 pages, 3s. 6d. net.

———— SEED CORN FOR THE SOWER. Compiled by Rev. C. H. PERREN, D.D. Fifth Edition. 394 pages, 3s. 6d. net; by post 3s. 11d.
THE METHODIST TIMES.—"An admirable collection of thoughts and illustrations."

PEARSON. AM I FIT TO TAKE THE LORD'S SUPPER? By Rev. SAMUEL PEARSON, M.A. Nineteenth Thousand. 16 pages, paper, 1d.; post free 1½d. 6s. per 100.

PHELPS. THE STILL HOUR. By Rev. AUSTIN PHELPS.
[See Sanctuary Booklets.

PHILLIPS. CHRISTIAN CHIVALRY. A Missionary Address to Young Men. By THOMAS PHILLIPS, B.A. Paper, 3d

PIERCE. THE DOMINION OF CHRIST. Sermons on Missionary Work. By Rev. W. PIERCE. 1s. 6d. net.

———— **AND HORNE.** PRIMER OF CHURCH FELLOWSHIP. 6d. and 1s. net. [See under Horne.

PORTER. THE CHRISTIAN SCIENCE OF LIFE. Letters to a Friend on the Old Faith in relation to the New Thought. By Mrs HORACE PORTER. Third Edition. 1s. 6d. net; paper, 1s. net; postage 2d. extra.
———— THE CHRISTIAN SCIENCE OF PRAYER. 1s. 6d. net; postage 3d. Second Edition.
———— THE VALLEY OF VISION. Some Glimpses of Things Unseen. 3s 6d. net.
THE CHURCH TIMES.—"By the Author of 'The Christian Science of Life,' and is written to illustrate the arguments admirably presented in that work. It reveals also the weak side of some 'faith-healing,' and all is done by a pleasant story about pleasant people."

POSTGATE. MISS TABITHA'S TRIAL, and other Stories for Mothers' Meetings. By ISA J. POSTGATE. 1s. 6d. net.
CHURCH TIMES.—" No child has keener zest for a story than the cheerful British housewife on her weekly outing to the mothers' meeting. These tales cannot fail to gain her entire approbation."

PRATT. THE WINGLESS ANGEL. Parables and Pictures. By the Rev. BERTRAM PRATT, M.A. 2s. 6d. net.
CHRISTIAN HERALD.—" Very bright and helpful; full of cheery suggestions; a sunny book for a foggy day."

———— VISIONS IN THE VALE. By the Rev. BERTRAM PRATT, M.A. 2s. net.

PRAYERS FOR HEALING. From the Ancient Liturgies and other Offices of the Church. Compiled by E. B. H. 1s. net; by post 1s. 2d.

PREACHER'S TREASURY, THE. Comprising "Points for Preachers and Teachers," "Seeds and Saplings," and "Little Sermons to the Children," bound together in one volume. 2s. 6d. net; by post 2s. 10d.
CHRISTIAN WORLD.—" A useful stand-by. The outlines are simple and suggestive.

REANEY. TEMPERANCE SKETCHES FROM LIFE. By Mrs G. S. REANEY. 1s. 6d. net; postage 4d.
HOME MISSION WORKER.—" The book for your moderate drinking friend."

RICHARDS. THE GOLDEN WINDOWS. A Book of Fables for Young and Old. By LAURA E. RICHARDS. 3s. 6d. net; postage 4d. Twenty-eighth Edition.

———— THE SILVER CROWN. Forty-five Parables. By LAURA E. RICHARDS. 3s. 6d. net; postage 4d. Fourteenth Edition.

———— FIVE-MINUTE STORIES. 101 Short Stories and Poems. By LAURA E. RICHARDS. With numerous illustrations. 5s. net. Fourth Edition.
THE CHURCH TIMES.—" ' Five-Minute Stories ' is one of those volumes which the relatives of young folk are glad to fall back upon when the request ' Please, do tell us another story' finds them at a loss."
BRITISH WEEKLY.—" Every variety of story is to be found in this volume, to suit every mood of every child."

ROBERTS. THE WAY OF VICTORY. Meditations and Verses for Lent, Passiontide and Easter. By Miss JEAN ROBERTS. [See Heart and Life Booklets.

ROBERTSON. THE LONELINESS AND SINLESSNESS OF CHRIST. By F. W. ROBERTSON. [See Heart and Life Booklets.
This is a word of good cheer from one of the greatest of preachers. For a friend in any distress of mind or soul no more helpful message could be found.

———— WORDSWORTH. A Lecture. By F. W. ROBERTSON. Paper, 6d. net; cloth, 1s. net; postage 1d.

———— TEN SERMONS. By F. W. ROBERTSON. Paper. 6d. net.

———— ELEVEN SERMONS. By F. W. ROBERTSON. A Second Selection. Paper, 6d. net.

———— TWELVE SERMONS. By F. W. ROBERTSON. A Third Selection. Paper, 6d. net.

———— THE INFLUENCE OF POETRY. Two Lectures on. By F. W. ROBERTSON. Crown 8vo, cloth, 2s. 6d. net.

ROBINSON. ANGEL VOICES. Twenty-four Addresses to Children. By Rev. W. VENIS ROBINSON, B.A. 2s. 6d. net; postage 3d.

ROGERS. THE JOY OF THE RELIGIOUS. By the Rev. EDGAR ROGERS. Cloth, 6d. net; postage 1d.
EXAMINER.—" Full of devout and holy thoughts, tinged with the mysticism of the Middle Ages."

ROLLINGS. THE GREAT ASSIZE. War Studies in the Light of Christian Ideals. By WILLIAM SWIFT ROLLINGS, Auckland, New Zealand. 3s. 6d. net; by post 3s. 10d. Strongly recommended by Dr CLIFFORD.

ROTHERHAM. LET US KEEP THE FEAST. Plain Chapters on the Lord's Supper. By J. B. ROTHERHAM. 1s. net; by post 1s. 1d.

———— CHRISTIAN MINISTRY. By J. B. ROTHERHAM. 2s. net; postage 2d.

———— STUDIES IN THE BOOK OF PSALMS. By J. B. ROTHERHAM. Demy 8vo, cloth, 10s. 6d. net.

RUSKIN. SESAME AND LILIES. By John Ruskin. Paper, 6d. net ; by post 8d. Reprinted from the original edition, unabridged. 1. OF KING'S TREASURES 2. OF QUEEN'S GARDENS.

——— "UNTO THIS LAST." Four Essays on the First Principles of Political Economy. By John Ruskin. Paper, 6d. net ; by post 8d.

——— THE MIRROR OF THE SOUL and other Noble Passages from Ruskin. Dainty wrappers, 6d net ; also in rich cloth gilt, 1s. net ; postage 1d. extra.

RUTHERFORD. THE UPWARD WAY. Readings for 31 days from Samuel Rutherford. Compiled by Miss Gregory. [See Heart and Life Booklets.

THE SANCTUARY BOOKLETS.

Tiny copies of famous books. Will go easily into a vest pocket. 32mo, cloth, 6d. net ; leather, 1s. net each ; velvet persian yapp, 1s. 6d. net each ; postage 1d.

THE PRACTICE OF THE PRESENCE OF GOD. By Brother Lawrence.

THE DREAM OF GERONTIUS. By Cardinal Newman.

ST PAUL. By Frederic W. H. Myers.

THE CHANGED CROSS. By the Honble. Mrs Hobart Hampden.

THE STILL HOUR. By Austin Phelps.

THE GOLDEN ALPHABET OF S. BONAVENTURA.

THE PRIVATE DEVOTIONS OF BISHOP ANDREWES.

EXCLAMATIONS OF THE SOUL TO GOD. By Saint Teresa.

THE RHYTHM OF BERNARD OF MORLAIX. Translated by the late John Mason Neale.

THE BOW IN THE CLOUD. Words of Comfort for Hours of Sorrow. By Dr J. R. Macduff.

THE MORNING WATCHES. By Dr J. R. Macduff.

THE NIGHT WATCHES. By Dr J. R. Macduff.

THE CHARACTER OF JESUS. By Horace Bushnell, D.D.

THE SAYINGS OF BROTHER GILES. Edited by Cardinal Manning. " Dainty volumes indeed, of a size to go into the vest pocket. There is nothing more suitable to take the place of a complimentary card than some of the world's devotional masterpieces issued by this firm in so pleasing and dainty a form. A card will soon be thrown away, these will be always treasured and used."

ST FRANCIS. LITTLE FLOWERS OF ST FRANCES OF ASSISI. First Twenty Books. [See Heart and Life Booklets.

——— LITTLE FLOWERS OF ST FRANCIS. India paper. 416 pages, leather, 2s. 6d. net ; velvet calf, gilt edges, 3s. 6d. net ; postage 2d.

SAUNDERS. CHATS WITH BOYS. By A. V. Saunders. 1s. net ; postage 2d.

SETH-SMITH. THE WAY OF LITTLE GIDDING. By E. K. Seth-Smith. 3s. 6d. net ; by post 3s. 11d.

SHEFFIELD. A DAUGHTER OF THE SLUMS. By Emma Sheffield. 1s. 6d. net ; postage 3d.

SHEPHEARD-WALWYN. LOOK STRAIGHT AHEAD. and other Talks with Boys and Boy Scouts. By Rev. E. W. Shepheard-Walwyn. 2s. net.

SINCLAIR. BIBLE OCCUPATIONS. Addresses by the Rev. George Sinclair, Glasgow. Two Series. 2s. net each.

ALLENSON'S VALUABLE SIXPENNY BOOKS.

Well printed in large clear type on good paper. Demy 8vo.

METHODIST TIMES.—"Mr Allenson is doing a good service by his sixpenny reprints."

PRACTICAL APOLOGETICS.

CHARACTERISTICS OF THE GOSPEL MIRACLES. By Bishop WESTCOTT. 6d. net; also cloth, 1s. net.

THE GOSPEL OF THE RESURRECTION. By Bishop WESTCOTT. 6d. net; cloth, 1s. net.

By Prof. A. W. MOMERIE.
PERSONALITY. 6d. net.
INSPIRATION. 6d. net.
THE ORIGIN OF EVIL. 6d. net.
IMMORTALITY. 6d. net.
IN RELIEF OF DOUBT. By R. E. WELSH. New Introduction by the BISHOP OF LONDON. 70th thousand. 6d. net.
THE CHRIST OF HISTORY. By JOHN YOUNG, LL.D. 6d. net.
THE GIFTS OF CIVILISATION. By DEAN CHURCH. 6d. net.

BELIEF IN GOD. By A. W. MOMERIE. Twentieth thousand. 6d. net.

THE TRUE THEOLOGY. By J. T. FREETH. 6d. net.

ANTI-NUNQUAM. By J. WARSCHAUER. Third Edition. 6d. net. Cloth boards, 1s. net.

THE ATHEIST'S DILEMMA. By J. WARSCHAUER. 6d. net.

THE CHALLENGE TO CHRISTIAN MISSIONS. By R. E. WELSH, M.A. 6d. net.

WHAT IS CHRISTIANITY? By JAMES MARTINEAU. Demy 8vo, 6d. net. Inspiration, Infallibility, Rationalism, etc.

ROOT PRINCIPLES IN RATIONAL AND SPIRITUAL THINGS. By T. CHILD. 6d. net.

DEVOTION AND SERMONS.

A SERIOUS CALL TO A DEVOUT AND HOLY LIFE. By WILLIAM LAW. Complete. 6d. net. Cloth boards, 1s. net.

ENDEAVOURS AFTER THE CHRISTIAN LIFE. By JAMES MARTINEAU. Two series. 6d. net each. Cloth, complete, 1s. 6d. net.

CHRIST'S CONQUEST AND OTHER SERMONS. By Rev. CANON LIDDON. 6d. net.

ROBERTSON'S SERMONS. By F. W. ROBERTSON, of Brighton. Three Series, Ten, Eleven, and Twelve respectively. 6d. net each.

J. H. NEWMAN'S SERMONS. Twelve selected. 6d. net.

SPURGEON'S SERMONS. Ten of his best. 6d. net.

CLASSICS OF ENGLISH LITERATURE.

SESAME AND LILIES. By JOHN RUSKIN. 6d. net.
UNTO THIS LAST. By JOHN RUSKIN. 6d. net.

HEROES AND HERO WORSHIP. By T. CARLYLE. 6d. net.
SARTOR RESARTUS. By THOMAS CARLYLE. 6d. net.

ENGLISH TRAITS. By R. W. EMERSON, 6d. net.

WHOLESOME FICTION.

THE WIFE'S TRIALS. By EMMA JANE WORBOISE. 6d. net.

Separately by post 8d. each.

SMITH. MEASURING SUNSHINE. Addresses to Children. By Rev. FRANK SMITH, M.A., B.Sc. 1s. 6d. net: by post 1s. 9d. [*Second Edition.*

SNELL. WORDS TO CHILDREN. Twenty-six Addresses by Rev. B. J. SNELL, M.A., B.Sc. 2s. net.

——— THE GOOD FATHER. Twenty-six Addresses to Children. By the Rev. B. J. SNELL, M.A., B Sc. Second Edition. 2s. net.

SPURGEON. TEN SERMONS. By CHARLES H. SPURGEON. Paper, 6d. net; by post 8d.

STANTON. THE ESSENTIAL LIFE. Essays. By STEPHEN BERRIEN STANTON. 3s. 6d. net ; by post 3s. 10d.
METHODIST TIMES.—" Almost every line provokes meditation and admiration. Preachers would certainly find these essays repay reading."

STREET. THE GOLDEN KEY. A Day Book of Helpful Thoughts for Children. Compiled by Miss LILIAN STREET. 476 pp. 2s. 6d. net ; leather, 3s. 6d. net ; velvet calf, 6s. net.
The CHURCH TIMES says :—" There are many books which offer to older persons a few thoughts for the day. Miss Lilian Street has hit upon the thought of compiling such a book for children, and she has carried it out with skill and sound judgment. The short passages are chosen from a wide range of reading, they are excellently arranged. It is a book which may well be kept in mind when presents are being chosen."

TAULER'S LIFE, AND SERMONS. 6s. net. [See Winkworth.

TAYLOR. THE APOSTLE OF PATIENCE AND PRACTICE. By the Rev. F. J. TAYLOR, B.A. 2s. 6d. net.

TERENCE. BEHIND THE BLINDS. By VESTA TERENCE. 2s. 6d. net ; by post 2s. 9d.

TERESA, ST. EXCLAMATIONS OF THE SOUL TO GOD. By ST TERESA. [See Sanctuary Booklets.

THOMAS, H. ELWYN. MARTYRS OF HELL'S HIGHWAY. By Rev. H. ELWYN THOMAS. Preface and Appendix by Mrs JOSEPHINE BUTLER. Cheap ed. Paper, 1s. net ; cloth, 1s. 6d. net.
An Exposure of the White Slave Traffic. A necessary Book which every Mother should read.

THOMAS, EVAN. ST PAUL'S COMFORTERS. By the Rev. EVAN THOMAS. 1s. 6d. net.
Most suggestive chapters on Friendship.

TILESTON. GREAT SOULS AT PRAYER. Fourteen Centuries of Prayer, Praise, and Aspiration, from St Augustine to Christina Rossetti and R. L. Stevenson. Selected by M. W. TILESTON. Seventh thousand.
Pocket Edition, India paper, paste grain, 2s. 6d. net ; velvet persian yapp, in box, 3s. 6d. net ; Turkey morocco, 5s. net ; postage 2d.
Also demy 16mo, cloth, bevelled boards, red edges, 2s. 6d. net ; postage 3d. Choice limp, dark green lambskin, gilt edges, 4s. net ; postage 3d.
SCOTSMAN.—" Few books of devotion are so catholic, in the original sense of the word ; and it is small wonder to see the compilation so successful."

TIPPLE. SUNDAY MORNINGS AT NORWOOD. Twenty-two Sermons and Twenty-two Pulpit Prayers. By Rev. S. A. TIPPLE. 3s. 6d. net ; postage 5d. [*Fifth Edition.*

TRENCH. WITH FRIENDS UNSEEN. Thoughts for those in Sorrow. Compiled by VIOLET TRENCH. 1s. net ; by post 1s. 1d.

TUNNICLIFF. WET PAINT. Twenty " Sermons in Signs " for Children. By the Rev. H. G. TUNNICLIFF. 1s. net ; postage 2d.
S.S. TIMES.—" A score of bright addresses, brief, helpful, practical."

——— MIND THE STEP. Thirty Sermons in Signs for Girls and Boys. Crown 8vo, 2s. 6d. net ; by post 2s. 10d.

——— THE KING'S SCOUT. Twenty-one Talks with Children. By Rev H. G. TUNNICLIFF. 1s. net.
Very freshly told Bible stories.

TYNDALL. OBJECT SERMONS IN OUTLINE. Forty-five Topics for Children's Services and P.S.A.'s, attracting the eye as well as the ear. By C. H. TYNDALL, M.A. 2s. 6d. net.

UFFEN. JACK AND THE GYPSIES, and other Stories I have told the Children. By J. M'CLUNE UFFEN. 2s. 6d. net.

UPHAM. THE LIFE OF MADAME GUYON. By T. C. UPHAM. 516
pages, 6s. net.   *[Third Edition.*
CHURCH QUARTERLY REVIEW.—" A most welcome reprint."

VARLEY. POINTS FOR PREACHERS AND TEACHERS. Illustrations
and Anecdotes. Compiled by G. W. VARLEY. 1s. net ; post free 1s. 2d. *[Second Edition.*

WARSCHAUER. THE ATHEIST'S DILEMMA. Paper, 6d. net. The
opening Lecture on "Theism or Atheism"; by Dr WARSCHAUER, in debate with Mr G.
W FOOTE.

———— ANTI-NUNQUAM. By J. WARSCHAUER, M.A., D.Phil. Reply to
Blatchford. Paper, 6d. net ; by post 8d. Cloth, 1s. net ; post free 1s. 3d.

WATSON. FORMATION OF CHARACTER. By Rev. J. B. S. WATSON,
M.A. Third Edition. 2s. net ; by post 2s. 4d.

WAYNE. READINGS FOR MOTHERS. By Mrs EDWARD WAYNE.
1s. net ; by post. 1s. 2d.

WEIR. WHAT JESUS TEACHES. Lessons from the Gospels for Girls
of To-day. By MARY ROSS WEIR. 1s. 6d. net.

WELLER. SUNDAY GLEAMS. Chats with the King's Children. By
the Rev. A. G. WELLER. 1s. 6d. net ; by post 1s. 9d.
A series of fifty outline Talks to Young People.

WELSH. GOD'S GENTLEMEN. Vigorous Sermons to Young Men.
By Prof. R. E. WELSH, M.A., D.D. Sixth Edition. 3s. 6d. net.
BRITISH WEEKLY.—" A frank and manly book."

———— IN RELIEF OF DOUBT. By Prof. R. E. WELSH, M.A., D.D.
Seventieth thousand. Paper, 6d. net ; by post 8d.
BRITISH WEEKLY.—" One of the best books of popular apologetics ever written."

———— THE CHALLENGE TO CHRISTIAN MISSIONS. By R. E.
WELSH, M.A. Second Edition. Crown 8vo, cloth, 2s. 6d. net. Also cheap Popular
Edition. 14,000 already sold. Paper, 6d. net ; by post 8d.
CHURCH MISSIONARY INTELLIGENCER.—" This book is undoubtedly the most important
attempt yet made to meet current objections to Missions."

WESTCOTT. THE GOSPEL OF THE RESURRECTION. By Bishop
WESTCOTT. Paper, 6d. net ; by post 8d. Cloth, 1s. net ; by post 1s. 2d.
LOCAL PREACHERS' MAGAZINE.—" Here is an opportunity for students of slender means
to read for 6d. that luminous exhaustive work which has done so much to close the mouths
of cavillers at the great foundation truth of Christianity."

———— CHARACTERISTICS OF THE GOSPEL MIRACLES. By the
late Bishop WESTCOTT. Paper, 6d. net ; cloth, 1s. net ; by post 1s. 2d.
The BISHOP OF LONDON says :—" The object of these cheap editions is to bring true masterpieces within the reach of everyone. It is very refreshing to read again what perhaps the
greatest mind the Church has produced in our generation thought of miracles."

WINKWORTH. JOHN TAULER, HISTORY AND LIFE OF. With
twenty-five of his Sermons by SUSANNA WINKWORTH. 426 pages, 6s. net.
GLASGOW HERALD.—" Mr Allenson has conferred a service on all lovers of the mystics, by
this reissue of an excellent work."

WOOD. REMEMBER THE CHILDREN. One hundred Short Addresses
to Boys and Girls. By the Rev. JOHN WOOD, Cowdenbeath. 2s. net ; by post 2s. 4d.
A splendid series of suggestive talks. Many Striking illustrations.

———— ONE HUNDRED MORE TALKS WITH BOYS AND GIRLS.
By the Rev. JOHN WOOD, F.R.G.S. 2s. net.

WOODBURN. THE ULSTER SCOT, his Religion and History. By
JAMES BARKLEY WOODBURN, M.A. With Five Maps. 382 pages, 5s. net.
     [Second Edition.
BRITISH WEEKLY.—" A new and notable book. Mr Woodburn is a man of broad and
enlightened views, scrupulously fair and candid."

WORBOISE. THE WIFE'S TRIALS ; or, The Story of Lilian Grey. By
E. J. WORBOISE. 124 pages, paper, 6d. net ; by post 8d.

WRIGHTSON. NANCY : or, The Cloud with the Silver Lining. By Miss
ADA WRIGHTSON (Sister Ada). 1s. net.

WYNNE. WORDS TO HELP. Fifty-three Readings on Difficulties in
Faith and Practice. By the late Ven. G. R. WYNNE, D.D. 2s. 6d. net.
THE GUARDIAN.—" We gladly commend such a sensible book."

YOUNG. THE CHRIST OF HISTORY. By Rev. JOHN YOUNG, D.D.
Paper, 6d. net ; by post 8d.

www.ingramcontent.com/pod-product-compliance
Lightning Source LLC
Chambersburg PA
CBHW030347270326
41926CB00009B/994